Kundalini Awakening

Effective Methods to Awaken Your Third Eye

(Chakra Healing Strategies to Balance Life With Transcendental Mindfulness)

Franklin Priddy

Published By **Cathy Nedrow**

Franklin Priddy

All Rights Reserved

Kundalini Awakening: Effective Methods to Awaken Your Third Eye (Chakra Healing Strategies to Balance Life With Transcendental Mindfulness)

ISBN 978-1-7779883-1-9

No part of this guidebook shall be reproduced in any form without permission in writing from the publisher except in the case of brief quotations embodied in critical articles or reviews.

Legal & Disclaimer

The information contained in this book is not designed to replace or take the place of any form of medicine or professional medical advice. The information in this book has been provided for educational & entertainment purposes only.

The information contained in this book has been compiled from sources deemed reliable, and it is accurate to the best of the Author's knowledge; however, the Author cannot guarantee its accuracy and validity and cannot be held liable for any errors or omissions. Changes are periodically made to this book. You must consult your doctor or get professional medical advice before using any of the suggested remedies, techniques, or information in this book.

Upon using the information contained in this book, you agree to hold harmless the Author from and against any damages, costs, and expenses, including any legal fees potentially resulting from the application of any of the information provided by this guide. This disclaimer applies to any damages or injury caused by the use and application, whether directly or indirectly, of any advice or information presented, whether for breach of contract, tort, negligence, personal injury, criminal intent, or under any other cause of action.

You agree to accept all risks of using the information presented inside this book. You need to consult a professional medical practitioner in order to ensure you are both able and healthy enough to participate in this program.

Table Of Contents

Chapter 1: The Third Eye Chakra 1

Chapter 2: The Third Eye and Psychic Abilities 13

Chapter 3: Exploring The Spirit World 40

Chapter 4: Seeing Other Worlds through the Third Eye 59

Chapter 5: History of Kundalini Yoga Philosophy 86

Chapter 6: What Is Kundalini Yoga, and What Are its Goals 97

Chapter 7: What Is Kundalini and What It Wakens 122

Chapter 8: Kundalini Yoga the Supreme Knowledge 131

Chapter 9: Physical, Mental and Sexual Benefits of Kundalini Yoga Practice 150

Chapter 10: What Are the Chakras? 164

Chapter 1: The Third Eye Chakra

Inside your body, positioned along or near your spine out of your tailbone to the pinnacle of your head, are your seven internal chakras. Your Third Eye Chakra is in the center of your forehead, among your physical eyes. Your frame will speak on a diffused stage with all of the energies spherical you. Certain of these energies will proper now relate to a particular a part of your frame. Of the seven inner chakras, the sixth in line is the Third Eye chakra. It right now correlates to your mental abilities, highbrow abilities, and how you examine your attitudes and beliefs. This chakra is installed right away on your pineal gland, pituitary gland, and your mind. This chakra is related for your mind. It is liable for your unconscious and aware intellectual tendencies as it resonates with the power of your psyche.

It is the chakra that homes your sixth experience, knowledge, and intuition.

Location and Function of the Third Eye Chakra

Everyone has a Third Eye chakra, and surely every body can open and get entry to their Third Eye chakra in the event that they select to perform that. You is probably using it with out even expertise which you are. Whenever you get that little feeling that a few factor isn't quite right with someone or a scenario, at the same time as your intestine tells you something you find hard to disregard, then that is your sixth revel in in motion. Your Third Eye is supplying you with the perceptions it has accrued so that you may additionally act upon this records. Even in case you are not proper away capable of discover the deliver of this records, it is though valid and ought to now not be unnoticed.

The Third Eye chakra is challenged with the resource of the need to discriminate a number of the supply of your mind and emotions, and whether or now not or not those are endorsed via illusion, worry, or strength. You will need to increase a thoughts this is impersonal and find the functionality to detach your self from highbrow and physical illusions. To be able to understand what's to your soul, you'll want to go beyond your thoughts, fears, and issues. Your Third Eye chakra will force all of those talents. It holds a mixture of reminiscences, personal opinions, fears, and statistics which can be all particular to you and your evaluations. All of those are generally lively inside the power of your diffused body, which is also referred to as your soul.

The foundation of all of the data you'll ever private lives in your Third Eye chakra. It deciphers the distinction amongst what's real and what you accept as true with to be real in any state of affairs. Negative reminiscences can appear indoors your mind and grow to be truths in your later lifestyles. If an character informed your little one self which you were silly, your man or woman self could most in all likelihood consider which you are a stupid individual. This example is just one instance of a feel that is valid to you, irrespective of the reality that you could't produce the facts to assist your concept. Your Third Eye is every distinctive sense organ that can be advanced with art work, and one of the matters that it's going to do is assist you dig via your evaluations to locate the statistics inside the again of them. It may also even assist you get maintain of the vibrations that exceptional people do away with, and this could help to enhance your perceptions of existence as you discover ways to choose out who to be with and who to place apart. The individual who made you experience silly via calling you silly might be the sort of you could set apart, or at least you can understand a way to cope with them in the destiny.

Your Third Eye chakra exhibits its basis in reality. Many of the ideas which you presently don't forget as truths aren't whatever greater than the remnants of preceding poor experience, like being cautioned you're stupid. Once you have got opened your Third Eye and may see the actual truth, then you will be able to rid your self of these wrong preconceived notions. This chakra desires to damage down the stereotypical thoughts you're keeping on to. The worldwide feeds you illusions, and you may be capable of detach your self from them. Your freedom will will will let you anticipate freely and manage your thoughts. There can be no limitations that you could now not have the capacity to overcome when this chakra is opened.

You will studies that there's no person character or company of human beings in society as a way to have the energy to decide the course that you will walk. A huge karmic entity will now stress your life and your selections. Until you may use the general electricity of your Third Eye chakra, you'll probably don't forget that the findings and opinions of diverse humans are the keys that pressure your movements, but that is only a psychic phantasm supposed to keep you as a captive in situations that aren't wholesome for you. Currently, you create karmic manifestations that reason you to be troubled by way of ailments or feel ache on your life. The beginning of your Third Eye will help you waft past all of that.

Psychic Abilities

Not anybody is privy to the manner to apply their psychic skills, specially in maturity, even though all of us is born with the know-how. Children see and sense the entirety due to the truth they've got no longer but located that there wishes to be barriers on what they could see, pay attention, and contact. Once children become adults, they usually lose the functionality to faucet into their psychic powers because their minds have come to be closed and jaded. Life's reviews have taught adults to distrust their private higher judgment, to the factor that they'll be slightly able to function on their non-public in the actual worldwide.

People who use their psychic talents daily are not any wonderful from you; they have got certainly determined out the manner to have an instinct that is going past the limits that define the bodily worldwide; they could flavor, experience, revel in, concentrate, and see topics that maximum human beings aren't capable of recognize. Most people have what's deemed to be the everyday perception by means of way of the recommendations of society. For maximum people in most conditions, the perception of reality is a actual rely. You can inform while a person isn't feeling nicely bodily, and you'll receive as real with most humans that the sky is blue with white fluffy clouds. When you start to extend your sensory capabilities, you could discover that most people do no longer use the various senses which is probably available to be used. You turns into greater aware of your inherently particular psychic objects at the identical time as you come to this attention.

Psychic abilties are the capability to method the sensory statistics that comes from each intangible and tangible assets. You will find out yourself able to approach this information on an immoderate spiritual, bodily, or emotional degree. This is a huge definition due to the fact psychic gives normally have a tendency to vary appreciably of their software program and intensity. You will experience a feel of oneness with the Universe on the equal time as you open your Third Eye chakra and use it regularly. The crucial recognition of some of the religious practices is achieving this oneness because of the truth then you'll have unlocked the powers of your Third Eye and your psychic talents.

Telepathic Awareness

When your Third Eye chakra is open, you may be able to get keep of mind or feelings from every distinctive character over distances, and that is known as telepathy. Using telepathy does now not contain the usage of the number one 5 senses of sound, sight, contact, perfume, or taste. With ESP, you apprehend some factor while now not having direct touch with it. Everyone is born with the capability to be telepathic, just like everybody is born with the strength of psychic abilities, but it takes conscious attempt to hold the ones competencies in use. Many human beings are not capable of learn how to use their telepathic powers because of the reality they view telepathy with mistrust and skepticism, and this maintains them from being absolutely capable of increase their talents.

You should be nicely cushty while you are trying to use your telepathic capabilities to talk with others. Your mind will want to be open and receptive to receiving records. If you maintain running toward your abilities at receiving messages from others and sending messages out to at least one-of-a-type humans, you can in the long run be able to do it with minimal attempt. Envision the recipient popularity with you and having a regular conversation, and use terms and terms that display exceptional element. Keep looking to ship out your message until you feel that it is been obtained. As you practice more, you will become familiar with this experience, and you may recognize even as your meant recipient has gotten the message you are sending. When you first begin receiving notifications, they will appear as surprising mind, and also you might be tempted to ignore them. Listen to the ones messages, even in case you don't act on them, due to the truth that is the start of the strains of telepathic verbal exchange setting out for you. News will come to you in numerous approaches. You also can collect emotions, thoughts, photographs, emotions, and dreams, and people are all everyday and recommend that the opposite character is sending messages which is probably whole of notable detail. Sometimes humans can get hold of notices whilst they're asleep.

When you begin the usage of your powers of telepathy to ship and benefit messages to at least one-of-a-kind human beings, you'll start to speak with other people on a deeper and more considerable degree. You will discover you have got were given a extra expertise of others. And this shape of conversation will paintings anywhere and each time, in any state of affairs, so it makes revel in as a way to increase this capability. When you grow to be more assertive to your workout, you can even learn how to block those human beings from whom you don't want to achieve any messages.

Chapter 2: The Third Eye and Psychic Abilities

Inside your physical frame is your diffused frame, the spiritual a part of you that receives messages from the Universe and sends messages again out. Your Third Eye chakra is what is accountable for your imagination, clairvoyance, focus, intuition, and psychic talents. To get preserve of the energies of the Universe, you will want to open your Third Eye and be in reality associated with it. This chakra is at the very middle of your 6th experience and the supply of all your psychic powers.

Your 6th experience is the instinct that lets in you to take a look at the future as well as the beyond and the prevailing. It will let you get hold of non-verbal messages from the alternative component of the veil, that cosmic shielding that separates the residing international from the area of the non-living. You gets keep of messages from loved ones who have lengthy lengthy gone on in advance than you, angels, and spirit publications. You can even use your Third Eye while there may be an purpose which you want to take place for your existence. A motive is an concept or a preference, and displaying simply way to make it a truth in your life. Your goal is probably to lose twenty pounds, and the manifestation is while you're taking steps to lose that twenty pounds. You will use your Third Eye to visualize your purpose, to peer it as being a part of truth.

Except for the Heart Chakra, this is the center chakra and the stability between the decrease 3 and the pinnacle three chakras, the chakras all have balancing chakras in your diffused body. The balancing chakra for the Third Eye is the Solar Plexus chakra, the middle of your intestine emotions. When the ones chakras are opened and balanced, they'll artwork collectively to enable you to cruise freely and effortlessly via your existence. You will despite the fact that come across hard times and one-of-a-type limitations alongside the way, but those are really the steps to your private and spiritual boom. Even even as you experience troubles, you will be capable of test from them speedy and expand and flow into on, without locating yourself caught in that unique state of affairs for extremely lengthy. When this chakra is open, it will come up with the strength to have a strong instinct, spiritual popularity, and intellectual readability.

ESP (Extra Sensory Perception)

This capability lets in you to acquire statistics alongside side your thoughts. This will include the abilties of telepathy, instinct, psychometry, clairvoyance, precognition, and retrocognition. There is likewise the capability that is referred to as the second one sight, in which you will in all likelihood studies matters that are not effortlessly available on your 5 senses; you may likely accumulate know-how thru a imaginative and prescient or a dream america. ESP is your 6th enjoy, the energy of your Third Eye. You will experience records in your intestine as well as in your soul and your coronary heart on the equal time as you are receiving facts using ESP. This form of psychic electricity, like the others, has no boundaries of time or location. You is probably able to manage bodily gadgets, see into the future, and realise the thoughts of other human beings. You also can additionally revel in ESP in lots of precise methods.

Precognition – This is the ability to take a look at the destiny route so that you will understand people, places, and sports activities in advance than they ever seem.

Retrocognition — This is the complete opposite of precognition, as it lets in you to investigate the beyond, and specially into the far off past. You is probably capable of understand beyond sports and those which you have been now not part of in actual-time.

Déjà vu — This includes feeling much like the latest experience which you are having is an experience that you have taken part in earlier than. With this form of ESP, you will understand the information of sports you have to not be able to recognize.

Telepathy — This is the strength that permits you to recognise the thoughts of different people. This capacity may be used to speak with others with out ever writing or talking.

Telekinesis — This is the electricity to physical have an impact on an object through the use of using the competencies of your mind, without ever touching the item.

Mediumship – This is the only capability that most human beings refuse to apply as it includes talking with deceased entities. Mediums channel the electricity of the departed and collect messages from them, and then they relay those messages to the folks which are organized right right right here inside the global of the residing.

Relaxation and Emptying the Mind

The idea of emptiness is a few different way to take a look at an revel in that you are having, a wonderful way to apprehend topics that will help you recognize them. Emptiness will no longer subtract from or upload to the actual raw records of the revel in. It will permit you to use your thoughts and your senses to make conclusions without questioning if there may be any backstory or personal data.

This type of wondering is known as emptiness as it has now not one of the suggestions that people commonly upload to an revel in to try to make enjoy of the enjoy. It allows you to look the area as it's far and to make sense of the activities of the arena which you stay. People will regularly create mythical memories to try to provide an cause of an occasion or revel in that they do now not understand, but emptiness will get rid of that addiction. When you create a view of the sector to explain an adventure, you interfere with the understanding and your capability to recognize it and remedy it, because your interest is drawn far from the essential information that you want.

When you undertake the practice of relaxing and emptying your thoughts, then you'll be capable of view an revel in or an occasion without reacting to it. You will watch the event because it takes region, and you could revel in no emotions in what you are seeing. You will surely try to decide what the occasion way for your existence if it has any because of this the least bit. Not all of existence's memories and sports may have a feel for your life, and emptying your mind will will let you decide which research warrant similarly interest from you. You will see the reality inside the event without feeling emotions.

It will take you time and workout to master the artwork of emptying your thoughts and getting to know to relax. The first intuition of maximum human beings, once they face a trendy experience or occasion, is to react to the state of affairs without delay. You will want to learn how to remove yourself from reaction and recognition on viewing what is taking area. Spend some time every day; recognition on the mind and perceptions that you hold as truths. See which of your mind you could get rid of, because of the truth this will assist you empty your mind, and a smooth thoughts is a snug mind. Lose your preconceived notions and assumptions about your views and tales. Removing the ones out of your thoughts will eliminate suffering and pressure on the grounds that it will in all likelihood be removing anger, greed, and delusions. Your thoughts might be clean, unfastened from the garbage this is restricting your psychic competencies.

Parallel Worlds

When you have have been given activated your Third Eye chakra and your psychic powers are wholesome, you'll be able to have interaction with entities in parallel worlds. These worlds do exist, and those entities already interact with human beings on Earth. There is essential proof that factors to the life of parallel worlds. In the area of quantum physics, it's miles advised that every viable outcome of a selected scenario will get up. Still, they'll all arise on unique planes and in top notch Universes. Only one end can rise up in each Universe. To allow this concept to be a reality, there need to need to be as many parallel worlds as there are feasible effects to a scenario. There is also the concept of the multiverse in physics. If we recollect that our Universe began out with the Big Bang, then it is feasible to suppose that many exclusive Universes commenced out with a comparable Big Bang. While some human beings say there's no concrete proof that other worlds exist, there's additionally no massive evidence that proves they do no longer exist.

In the middle of your physical brain, there may be a small gland, about the shape and period of a small pine cone that is called the pineal gland. Ancient instructors believed that the pineal gland changed into surrounded with the aid of a substance that modified into similar to vapor and emerge as the point of get entry to into the soul of the human. We apprehend now that the pineal gland is part of your endocrine gadget, and its method is to secrete the hormone melatonin, the hormone that is responsible for controlling your circadian rhythms, those regular cycles of sleeping and being conscious this is ruled with the aid of the presence or absence of moderate and dark. The pineal gland does not produce melatonin whilst there may be discernible mild, so people sleep at night time and stay awake within the daylight hours. The melatonin that the pineal gland secretes is the hormone that induces sleep.

Mystics and seers once reputable the pineal gland because of the reality they believed that it had some manipulate over the Third Eye chakra. Since they observed that light and darkish guided the human in their drowsing and waking, and considering the fact that they knew that all access into the human soul got here via the vapor surrounding the pineal gland, they believed that the pineal gland changed into in a few way worried with bringing statistics from outdoor the mind to the soul internal of the frame. The pineal gland is a sensor that specializes in detecting the adjustments outdoor your frame and makes the vital internal adjustments to make physiological changes. The pineal gland offers you the feeling of nicely-being at the same time as it works harmoniously together with your Third Eye so you revel in a heightened tendency in the direction of spirituality. Your Third Eye attaches you in your diffused frame, as it's miles the bridge a few of the spirit worldwide and you. Your Third Eye will see the fact this is beyond what your human eyes see, specifically in subjects referring to entities in parallel worlds. The doorway to all psychic and spiritual values is probably open to you, and you may be able to use lucid dreaming, telepathy, clairvoyance, and astral projection as you need.

Astral Mind Travel

Depending on the manner of existence that it's miles referring to, astral mind journey can pass through using many distinct names. Whether it's miles recognized with the resource of one of the western terms of dream frame, celestial frame, or strength frame; or the diamond body of Taoism, the Egyptian ka, the Buddhist moderate body, the diffused body of Tantric culture, the Hindu frame of bliss, or the Christian experience of the awesome heavens, it is all a form of astral thoughts journey. The human frame consists of the bodily shape and the diffused body, and it is your diffused body that is active on the identical time as you are dreaming and is responsible for projecting astrally. Your out-of-body evaluations are the combination of your goals and astral projection. When your subtle body is properly cultivated, then it will likely be capable of continue to exist the bodily frame as a model for cognizance.

Astral thoughts journey is likewise called an out-of-frame experience or OOBE. These may be intentional, or they might appear involuntarily whilst you're slumbering. You can also purpose an OOBE through depriving your self of water and food, or if you are unwell in any other case you be anxious via some bodily or intellectual trauma. Lucid dreams make outstanding possibilities for astral mind tour. You begin the experience with the useful resource of the use of looking at your slumbering shape after you've got were given left your body. Practice will can help you be capable of direct your attention to specific places or sports activities. Your subtle body is the location of your shape so that it will do the journeying. Your rational thoughts and your physical body are related to every different thru your subtle body, the intermediate body of mild that travels the astral planes. When your celestial body is having an OOBE, it's miles crossing the astral planes of diverse Universes.

Astral adventure furthermore validates the existence of life after the lack of existence of the physical body. When you have have been given revel in with astral excursion, you will be in fact aware about yourself outside of your bodily body. You can be able to touch, pay hobby, fragrance, see, and taste from the region around you. When you are deeply in meditation, soundly sleeping, or carrying out aware astral adventure, a switch is activated that permits you to tour on exceptional planes. This transfer is the activation of the pineal gland, which releases chemical substances that purpose your diffused frame to go away your physical body, whether or not you are consciously traveling astrally, deep into your meditation, having a lucid dream, or getting ready to lack of life. And having your Third Eye chakra open and healthy is important for all of this to take place.

Since your unconscious is on pinnacle of factors of your soul at the identical time as you are slumbering, you have not any quantity of manipulate over what takes area until you have got a lucid dream. If you are doing so, then you can have a heavenly thoughts experience and tour from your body. There are some blessings on the manner to exercise astral thoughts journey consciously. You can be able to excursion nicely beyond the boundaries of the bodily worldwide and its rational idea methods. Your inner religious being will blossom, and you can revel in a specific growth on your astral abilties. You can experience a whole transformation of your attitude of your self as a religious and physical being in this international. You would possibly locate that you can characteristic with a more revel in of attention in the day by day sports sports of your lifestyles while you enjoy astral thoughts journey. The cause for that is which you are definitely solid in the information which you are greater than simplest an insignificant bodily being who's doomed to stay a humdrum life and be forgotten after dying.

It is fairly smooth to prepare your body to have a heavenly thoughts journey revel in. This is regularly best finished within the early hours of the morning due to the fact it is simpler for you to reach the comfortable kingdom of being and heightened awareness that is desired. This additionally may be completed just earlier than you fall asleep for the night time time. Astral mind tour is a private experience, so have your enjoy at the identical time as the time is proper for you. Do this at the same time as you get into bed considering the truth that your bodily frame will need to be without a doubt relaxed. And because of the fact astral thoughts journey is a private revel in, it's far extraordinary to prepare for it while you are on my own. Keep the room dark and silent and take away anything that might distract you.

Lie flat to your lower back and easy your mind. The reason is with a view to gain a country in which your mind and frame are completely comfortable. Breathe inner and out, slowly and lightly. Try no longer to recollect anything, both idea approximately your day or thoughts about the tour you are approximately to take. If you have a crystal to clean your Third Eye chakra, you can region it in your brow at the same time as you are thrilling. Let your bodily frame, and your subtle frame get close to the edge of sleep, however do now not allow yourself to doze off clearly but. For astral mind travel to get up, you may want to be at that thin line amongst being wide awake and being asleep. Keep your eyes actually closed, and your cognizance on one part of your frame. Try to make that component float via the usage of way of using best the power of your mind. Keep broadening your focus till you have were given blanketed your whole frame in your path. Continue until you could maintain forward along side your whole body via way of the use of the energy of your mind.

Now it's miles vitally crucial, more than ever earlier than, so one can continue to be comfortable because of the fact you'll possibly experience a chain of actions like little waves as your soul receives prepared to depart your body. If you revel in any worry at this 2d, your soul will not skip and you could no longer be able to interact in astral thoughts tour. Let the vibrations of the waves deliver you at the identical time as you continue to stay comfortable and non violent. Use the electricity of your mind yet again to move your body to a standing characteristic. As you get up, take a search around the room that your physical frame is mendacity in, then walk throughout the room and flip and test yourself, all at the same time as the use of truly the powers of your thoughts. If your bodily frame can revel in you looking at yourself from throughout the room, then your check have end up successful, and you're prepared for astral mind journey.

You can also moreover need some concrete evidence which you are engaged in astral mind excursion. Go into any other room and flow into an object, searching at it cautiously earlier than you area it back down. Then at the same time as you awaken, you could physical pass into the alternative room and find out that object. When you have have been given without a doubt mastered this method, then you definitely surely have mastered astral thoughts tour. Eventually, you can need to journey to new locations that are not as familiar to you. When you tour, continuously try and mentally report facts of the places wherein you pass, so that you can skip decrease again and look for those places later. When you use astral mind journey to visit unexpected locations, they may seem acquainted whilst your physical frame is going there. Astral thoughts journey is flawlessly secure, and you'll generally go again to in which to procure right here from.

Controlling your Dreams

You may additionally have already experienced a lucid dream. If you've got were given ever been dreaming, after which you suggested yourself that that is a dream because you've got been sure that you were dreaming, then that could be a lucid dream. If you have ever managed the storyline that the dream had, then this is moreover a lucid dream. Most humans dream all of the time and in no manner apprehend that they may be dreaming until they awaken and hold in thoughts components of the dream. Lucid desires seem at some point of periods of rapid eye motion, just like all one-of-a-type goals do.

Lucid goals commonly display up spontaneously, although it is viable to train your self to have a lucid dream. The potential of human beings to manipulate their dreams varies considerably. Lucid dreaming is a manner which will will permit you to explore the worlds which can be internal your mind even on the identical time as you're actually conscious that you are dreaming. There are many practical packages for the use of lucid dreaming in real-international conditions. One manner to use lucid dreaming is for human beings who have normal nightmares to seize manipulate of the nightmare and change its course consciously. You are a great deal much less probable to be scared of some element that you may manage. You can also use lucid dreaming as a form of leisure as it will will let you journey anywhere and do some thing which you want.

There are subjects that you may do if you want to exercise lucid dreaming. One method of attempting out your dreaming is referred to as fact trying out. This will help you to verify whether or not or not you're in a dream. While you're dreaming, take a look at the time on a clock, and recheck it severa minutes later. If you have got were given a lucid dream, the time will range wildly, not skip at a herbal tempo as it does even as you are huge extensive wakeful. For your dream to be considered a lucid dream, it's going to need to have four common traits. You will need to recognize which you are dreaming, the assets you observe on your dream may additionally additionally disappear while you wake up, your dream will not study any favored pointers of physical criminal recommendations, and also you apprehend that there may be every different international that is outdoor of the dream worldwide that you are in. The dream does no longer want to make sense; you really want that permits you to understand what goes on inside the dream. For example, in case you dream that you can flap your fingers and fly through the air and it makes sense to you inside the dream, then you definitely genuinely have a lucid dream. It doesn't be counted that human beings absolutely can't fly, due to the fact the bodily criminal tips of the actual global do now not look at inside the lucid dream.

Lucid goals artwork in four degrees, each one being extra profound than the step before. The first stage is the regular degree of non-lucid dreaming, in which maximum humans begin. When you're in this u . S ., you may haven't any concept that you are dreaming and something that you see, you will preserve in thoughts later and accept it as being part of truth. You will now not have any aware manipulate of your dream, and it will be completely comprised of your mind. In the second diploma, you could start dreaming of something that appears not possible within the center of dreaming about some element viable. Your unconscious thoughts is being blocked through some difficulty on your conscious thoughts, so on the identical time as you can need to depart the dream, you aren't able to. At this issue, you're in part aware which you are dreaming and pretty now not. When you acquire the 1/three diploma of lucid dreaming, you will be capable of have an wholly lucid dream as long as you're willing to clearly receive the lucid dream. You need to understand which you are in a dream and be organized to stay there and experience the dream. The maximum crucial part of the lucid dream isn't in control of the dream, but in being willing to play together with the dream. On the fourth degree, you may be capable of experience the stop of the dream, whether or not or not it entails a end or ends, and you may awaken.

Developing your Third Eye is your doorway to all feasible psychic research you may have. When this functionality is cultivated, then the separation among spirit and self will dissolve. You will revel in cynicism, jealousy, uncertainty, pessimism, and confusion if this chakra is blocked. The highest deliver of divine energy will come thru an open Third Eye. Opening this chakra will supply you the potential to engage in astral projection and lucid dreaming. This might also moreover give you an extra creativeness and a higher best of sleep.

Chapter 3: Exploring The Spirit World

The spirit international is that realm this is inhabited via spirits, the ones religious manifestations that inhabit other parallel worlds. This outside environment for souls is impartial of the natural global that you settle, however the herbal global and the spirit international are constantly interacting with every different. These worlds constantly talk with each one-of-a-kind thru diverse techniques.

There are many geographical areas of life past the physical worldwide in which you stay. The domain names carry out on super vibrational frequencies than this one because of the fact each detail is on a one in every of a type stage of strength. When you adventure some of the nation-states, you becomes aware about a change, a shift in the electricity from one usa to every other. The spirit geographical areas moreover do no longer feature just like the physical realm in which you live, wherein many specific human beings make a melting pot of humans and their trends. In the spirit global, every location is the area of spirits who have completed a particular degree in their spirituality. When humans depart this physical realm, they do no longer right away end up saints or angels. People who pass on will keep their character and memory, and they'll preserve in a lot the identical shape as they did after they were alive, but in one of the spirit nation-states.

When you go away this physical international, you could visit the vicinity which you need to visit, a plan that is based totally on the manner you lived your lifestyles in this realm. This level of spirituality might be pondered within the vibration of your aura. Your vibrations may be higher if you have been a spiritual individual in this realm. You will then skip into the area that maximum closely suits your vibrational stage. These population of these spirit geographical regions will go to your physical realm, and that they encourage verbal exchange among the domain names.

Clairvoyance

This phrase interprets into a clean imaginative and prescient. Clairvoyance is the functionality to take a look at records approximately a person, object, region, or event by means of using your psychic capabilities and further-sensory perceptions (ESP). People who use ESP are clairvoyants who use the strength of clean sight to look folks or events which can be in far flung time or area. There are 3 precise abilities that all fall underneath the umbrella of prophecy. Remote viewing is the notion of events which are presently taking region which is probably outdoor of your regular kind of belief, like sports that show up an extended way away. Precognition offers you the functionality to understand or are looking forward to destiny events, and retrocognition is the functionality to view activities which can be from the past.

Clairvoyants will see matters with their thoughts's eyes, the use of their 6th experience via their Third Eye chakra. The real understanding of the clairvoyant is the capacity to decide the because of this of a message or an photograph that they collect. This allows them to decipher the vibrations that one of a kind people emit in addition to achieve notifications from the spirit global. Many humans are clairvoyant with out knowing that they may be, but they may show positive trends or capabilities. If you have got got had been given intellectual photographs randomly flash into your mind, in case you see visions to your thoughts that look like a movie is playing or if you get flashing photos of numbers, shades, symbols, or particular pix, then you can have clairvoyant talents. This is specially actual in case you see flashes of colours or vibrant lights, as those may be angels or spirit publications trying to talk with you to send you a message. Since prophecy has hundreds to do with seeing intellectual or physical images, visualization is a huge a part of being clairvoyant.

You might be capable of accumulate an object without studying the path or restore a small gadget due to the fact you may see to your mind how the item want to operate. You should probably in no manner wander away due to the reality you've got a marvelously innate experience of path. You excel at assembling puzzles, finishing mazes, and analyzing maps because the responsibilities that require visible dispositions and spatial skills are your location of expertise. You prefer jobs that will let you use your sense of creativity, and you dearly love adorable subjects. Your desires are often sincerely extraordinary because of your overactive imagination. If you have got a number of the ones developments, or maybe if you don't but would really like to increase them, then you can perform a bit or all of the following bodily games.

Meditation – The exercise of meditation is important to being a clairvoyant and to starting your Third Eye chakra. When you workout your meditation frequently, you may develop your psychic objects and decorate the vision of your Third Eye. You can be able to easy your senses, enhance your vibration, and get out of your logical thoughts.

Keep a Dream Journal – Clairvoyants will normally have terrific dreams, and writing them down in a pocket ebook is an top notch way to make bigger your capabilities. When your logical mind is at relaxation, your subconscious mind takes over, just so it's miles loose to acquire messages from the spirit international. Sleep time can be a excellent time to play on the same time as your unconscious thoughts is making connections with the spirit worldwide and engaging in astral journey. It is a first rate concept if you want to hold your dream mag proper beside your mattress. This will will will permit you to write down your goals the instantaneous you awaken even as they'll be despite the fact that smooth for your mind. You also can plan to get keep of messages from the spirits by means of the use of using merely putting an intention at the same time as you are falling asleep.

Playing with Crystals – Crystals are useful to in truth every body who's on foot with their chakras, their air of mystery, or growing their psychic competencies. Use a crystal to open your Third eye, and to preserve it open and healthful. Put a crystal on a desk close to you at the same time as you're meditating, or hold it on your hand lightly. Put the crystal on the table next for your mattress whilst you sleep. While clean quartz will paintings on any chakra, a bit of amethyst or fluorite is each renowned for their functionality to heal your Third Eye chakra. Other real alternatives for crystal remedy for the Third Eye chakra are aquamarine, opal, emerald, and celestite.

Play Games that Encourage Clairvoyance – Simple video games will help you enhance your clairvoyant abilities on the same time as you are having fun playing them. Play the cardboard activity 'reminiscence.' To play this sport, you'll lay all of a deck of gambling cards face down, and then you may turn them over at a time, searching out pairs of the identical card. Have a family member or pal set a set of ten unrelated devices on a desk. Study the topics for one minute, and then leave the room. While you are lengthy past, the alternative man or woman will eliminate one of the devices and cover it from your view. When you come to the room, you can need to inform which object is missing.

Practice Visualization – the Clairvoyants, will need to have strong abilties for visualization, so this is one trait that you will need to exercise. Clairvoyants see with their thoughts's eye, their Third Eye, so all the visions, images, and logos which you see can be on your mind. You will discover it hundreds less difficult to collect photographs if your Third Eye is open and functioning effectively. Take a while every day to visualize top notch photos, scenes, and pictures in your mind. Relax even as you are doing this and try to have a laugh with it, using pictures to create pics on your mind.

Premonitions

Spirituality is based totally on the attention which you are linked to some element greater than yourself or your ego. This a few difficulty extra goes through many special names, depending at the ideals of the unique character. Religious human beings may additionally communicate with the better power because the Almighty, God, Yahweh, Buddha, or Allah. Those who aren't believers in one formal faith but bear in mind themselves spiritual creatures may communicate over with the Great Spirit, the Absolute, or the electricity in the Universe. And a few human beings don't test with any name the least bit but opt to don't forget the higher energy as a enjoy of limitless beauty and top notch order. Whether you label it or no longer, that something extra presents you with a revel in of because of this and electricity on your lifestyles.

As humans mature spiritually, they will often locate that their strength of knowledge and seeing expands. These improved competencies frequently encompass the functionality to understand sports which have now not but happened, occasions which can be within the destiny. There is an extended line of seers, shamans, visionaries, and prophets in an effort to attest to this opportunity. The modern-day model of this ability is now referred to as the 6th sense, gut feelings, instinct, or hunches.

Premonitions have a deep connection to spirituality, in particular whilst the suspicion involves someone we adore or care deeply about. Premonitions will open you as a lot as other human beings and the relaxation of the Universe. They display which you are part of some thing lots huge than your self, which you are an element within the fabric that connects all the beings to your Universe. Premonitions reveal the oneness that exists while minds are linked throughout time and area. They are proof which you are not an remoted man or woman, but someone whose person interest operates out of doors past your physical body. They suggest which you are infinite in time and area. Premonitions are the window thru which you could see your connection to the Divine.

You can take a look at your hunches to decide whether or now not or not or no longer your suspicions are actual. Before you realise who's calling at the cellular telephone, try to guess who the caller is. Try to expect what a store will seem like on the interior at the same time as you're nonetheless outdoor of the door. The functionality to realize those gadgets isn't always achievement; it's far premonition. When you enjoy déjà vu, do not be terrified of it because of the reality there may be not some thing scary about it. Déjà vu is simply telling you that you have statistics of this area or person in advance than you are bodily there, and that is a premonition. People regularly forget approximately that nagging feeling of their gut, but you want to now not, because of the reality this is just a suspicion that some detail approximately this man or woman or situation is not proper.

Many people will enjoy their premonitions at the same time as they'll be dreaming. They can see the folks that are concerned within the state of affairs and the state of affairs itself. This is referred to as having a premonitory dream. Your mind is showing you a few trouble for you to seem in the destiny in real life. If you may have this kind of vision, then you could be susceptible to sports that aren't with out difficulty explained in simple phrases. You are possibly greater intuitive and open-minded than most people you understand. The maximum big distinction between regular desires and premonitory dreams is that premonitory dreams are based on real situations. You will find out yourself in a scenario looking human beings do subjects, and it could be part of a dream, and it may be taking area in real life. In a vision, the events of the dream are made out of your thoughts, and you're on pinnacle of things of the activities of the dream. When you've got have been given a premonitory dream, the sports activities of the dream will come to you, and you'll genuinely watch them unfold, as despite the fact that you had been looking a movie on a display show. You will have no control over the dream. And those are smooth to keep in mind at the same time as you wake up because of the reality premonitory desires are informative and surely colourful.

There is a particular cause for your sixth experience being activated, as it is in a premonitory dream. The dream is attempting to present you information so that you will be privy to a coming situation and you may recognize what to do even as you stumble upon it. When you sleep, your mind is free from the restraints of the bodily worldwide, and it's far open to go in whichever path it chooses to move. If a selected premonitory dream keeps returning to you, it's miles satisfactory in case you pay interest, because your spirit guide is trying to inform you a few aspect.

Daydreams

The act of having a pipe dream is permitting a ordinary motion of aware thoughts to preserve you from doing those belongings you are presupposed to be doing, or it'd honestly be a way to skip the time pleasantly. It will direct your attention inward to private and inner subjects and away from the outdoor problems which might be surrounding you. Almost absolutely everyone daydreams, and no imaginations are ever equal in content cloth fabric. Fantasies serve to help you with considering the destiny, thinking creatively, and thinking of latest procedures to deal with vintage problems, clean your attention span, and thinking creatively.

Daydreaming is an extraordinary launch from boredom. Daydreaming will can help you permit your mind wander for the duration of the ones instances while you're engaged in some tedious challenge, or you are someplace you'll as a substitute now not be. Sometimes the stimulus coming in from out of doors is repetitive and reasons you to music it out with having a pipe dream. This helps you to relieve the stress to your mind with the aid of using mentally stepping some distance from the repetitive records so you can circulate lower returned to it at the same time as you need to. If you're facing severa precise issues on the same time, you would possibly need to daydream about one-of-a-kind consequences for the conditions. This will allow you to switch your mind amongst wonderful streams of facts when you have severa dreams you need to devise for. Creativity is extended in those who daydream, mainly in the ones those who daydream even as they're seeking to remedy a complex hassle. When you operate having a pipe dream about speculating about future sports, you will have the opportunity to plot your response to them and their feasible conclusions. This may additionally assist you maintain your mind off your goals on the equal time as you try to plan the route of motion that is the tremendous with a view to attain them.

Man has extended been interested by the workings and wanderings of the human thoughts. Your thoughts comes with a integrated default network considering the fact that it is made of precise structures, and all human brains are built the identical. The device in your thoughts will hyperlink numerous regions collectively to create sensory opinions. These testimonies cause the thoughts to endure in thoughts things which might be aside from the sports activities which can be coming into the thoughts from assets outside of the mind. Daydreams and fantasies are different phrases for the best workings and wanderings of your thoughts.

Daydreams aren't simply useful device to keep you from being bored, but they have got practical functions of serving. They will let you explore your internal mind and thoughts. Daydreams are especially beneficial while you are trying to ponder your past studies, developing snap shots of events you preference will display as much as you inside the destiny, looking to decipher the mind or actions of different people, or if you are confronted with an ethical or ethical preference.

Chapter 4: Seeing Other Worlds through the Third Eye

The astral aircraft, the area of the spirits, is inhabited with the aid of the spiritual manifestations of diverse entities, and it is referred to as the otherworldly environment for souls. This international is independent of the herbal international that human beings inhabit, notwithstanding the truth that those worlds regularly have interaction with every one of a kind. The entities of each worlds can talk with every specific all through the astral planes. Humans have been looking for answers for masses of years approximately the religious global. Man has discovered many unique procedures to hook up with and speak with the planets which might be beyond their very non-public to gain higher electricity and religious facts.

The Art of Divination

The capability to foretell foresees, expect, or collect concept from the spirit international or a divine electricity is divination. When you exercising divination, you are trying to benefit perception right into a query or a situation through soliciting for information via a particular exercise or ritual. You should make direct touch with a spirit or a god, or you can look at signs and signs and symptoms, activities, or omens. The technique at the back of divination is to systematically prepare all the disjointed or random facts of the scenario so you can use them to offer you with belief proper right into a situation or trouble.

Divination has been used by oracles and seers for hundreds of years to divine the truth from the spirit global. A prophet is someone who gives precognition or prediction the use of data that they received from the gods, to provide prophetic or insightful advocate to community leaders. The terms of the oracle were deemed to be the terms of the gods handed down for the leaders to act upon. Seers never spoke immediately with gods due to the reality the prophets did, however their activity modified into to interpret the signs and symptoms and signs and symptoms and symptoms the gods left for the human beings. The seers used all of the techniques at their disposal to reap statistics, but they could not provide sure solutions to the leaders because the oracles may additionally want to. Through the sight of their Third Eye, they had been capable of provide solutions to the destiny of man. Using know-how of beyond events and theories of future activities, a person training divination can provide insights into modern activities. When you have were given completely opened and engaged your Third Eye, there can be severa strategies of divination to be had a good manner to use.

Scrying has been used because of the truth that historic times, and it's miles one of the oldest strategies of divination this is to be had to use. The traditional image of someone running towards scrying is the vintage crone bending over her crystal ball. The phrase comes from phrases that suggest 'to show' or 'to make out.' So the exercise of scrying is all about revealing the matters which can be unseen via using your 2d sight and the strength of your Third Eye. Your 2nd sight will provide you with the ability to appearance some detail which can't usually be perceived by way of using the usage of the usage of your five senses.

Scrying will permit you to get in contact together with your unconscious mind and all the realms of your soul. It is a powerful form of reading your self and knowledge your intentions. Scrying is a lovely approach for getting into contact together together together with your maximum private desires, desires, and wishes if you are struggling collectively together with your motive, because of this, or direction in life. Scrying is usually completed through the use of a few reflective floor, but there are distinct techniques you may use for scrying. You can drip candle wax onto the water after which interpret the phrases or snap shots the wax drippings shape as they harden. Relax your imaginative and prescient and stare right proper right into a replicate, and then appearance earlier to the photos to appear to you. Stare right right into a frame of water after which have a examine the snap shots which you see there. Watch the flames of a roaring hearth or the smoke growing from the fireplace for shapes and images. Gaze up on the fluffy clouds floating within the sky and see what ideas and office work are found to you.

When you're scrying, it is essential so you can allow your mind wander however preserve your focus on the item, so it does require some quantity of workout to emerge as gifted at scrying. You need to allow your conscious thoughts to open and allow mind and emotions to glide freely via your Third Eye.

Dreaming of Symbols

Dreams are the messages that the better powers of the Universe send to you, and they'll frequently maintain symbols and pix with a purpose to bring you a particular that means that is applicable in the natural global. There is an limitless amount of symbols and pix that could come to you in your desires. Anything that you can dream about can convey you a extra profound mental and emotional enjoy and importance than the object or occasion itself. If you dream about a house, it could supply many particular meanings. A vicinity may additionally constitute somewhere which you used to stay, it is probably something you need to benefit for your life, or it would bring a greater profound because of this tied to an event on your earlier life revel in, in particular in your adolescents. Then you can have dreams in which you're exploring one-of-a-type houses in case you need to change a few element for your waking life. If you're craving the a good deal less difficult life you cherished as a infant, then you definately might in all likelihood dream approximately your adolescence home. The key to understanding what the residence is trying to tell you is tied in your response to the residence. If you're looking for exchange and also you dream approximately exploring homes, then the manner you react to the homes will inform you even as you need to preserve looking and if you have positioned what you're looking for. Images and emblems in dreams do no longer have truely one that means, however a few topics are so acquainted to look in desires that they have got received meanings which may be generally ultra-modern due to the fact the message they'll be bringing.

●A chase scene technique which you are retaining off a few detail vital to your existence; you are strolling faraway from a few factor or someone that you need to confront and treatment.

●Water is indicative of the emotional nation you are currently experiencing, whether the water is calm and peaceful or wild and crashing.

●Any type of car presentations an impediment that you need to stand or the direction you want your existence to visit.

●Different humans and precise kinds of humans on your goals are reflections of your persona traits.

●When you dream of being decrease returned in faculty, you are looking for training inside the sports out of your childhood.

●Dreaming about being paralyzed is an indication that you're feeling overwhelmed by way of some thing or someone on your existence, or that you are feeling you are tied to a selected person or situation.

●Dreaming about loss of existence is not an omen of factors to go back again, but an illustration that a few trouble on your life desires to forestall or go away.

●Flying in dreams is the correlation of the way you revel in your life is going. The way which you are flying is a direct indication of the cutting-edge route of your life, so flying out of control technique that you are feeling your existence is out of manage.

- Falling is frightening whenever, but to your dream, it's miles telling you that you need to permit move of some problem that you are setting at once to for your lifestyles.

- You may additionally additionally fear feeling inclined if you dream which you are naked in a public vicinity.

- Dreaming about having a infant does now not continuously mean which you need a infant; it commonly technique that you are searching out a few detail new and easy to your lifestyles.

- Food can mean such a whole lot of various subjects to your life. It may additionally mean you want nourishment on an emotional or spiritual degree. It might probable mean you are searching for expertise or strength, or new insights into the manner your life is going.

Etheric Entities

The potential to art work with the entities of the etheric worldwide is needed on your religious work. An entity of the etheric international is a being this is non-material and active. When you start your technique of awakening, you will have a extremely good choice for cutting-edge day records. This new focus will lead you via the darkness this is on the earthly aircraft and out the alternative aspect to the moderate of the alternative side. You will encounter the entities of the etheric as you search for the modern facts which you preference. These entities will substantially variety in their shape and strength. Their degree of power is right now associated with their recognition in the spirit global.

You ought to have the possibility to have interaction with many one-of-a-type types of etheric entities. You will stumble upon complex spirits, cultivated spirits, easy spirits, angels, disembodied human beings, and deities. The many aspects of the cosmos can be without delay reflected in the incredible entities of the etheric. The huge fields of attention and strength within the etheric realm are the deities. The numerous distinctive spirits are greater localized entities, and they're a smaller presence in the etheric realm. They can exchange their shape each time they want to. By interacting with the entities of the etheric, you may be capable of draw upon a larger collective of energy and awareness.

By beginning your Third Eye, Chakra, you will begin to boom the abilties that you will need to look those entities and talk with them at the same time as you desire.

To end up aware about their presence, you will use your etheric belief, and whilst you need to percentage with them, you may use your etheric communique. You can be able to determine the form of interplay that you can have with the entities of the etheric thru assessing the character of your personal goal, the shape of entity which you are interacting with, and the right courting that you have with that entity. Your subtle frame will determine the extent of the relationship that you could have with the entities of the etheric. Your dating may even rely upon the particular entity which you are accomplishing.

Cultivated entities are those clean creatures that have been created via unique strategies to cast power. They are also known as servitors, types of idea, or synthetic elements. When cultivated entities are sufficiently superior, they will be capable of showing the critical talents of the entities of the etheric. For motives of practicality, they'll frequently attach themselves to a material form. They decide on particular material forms collectively with paintings, clay figures, wax figures, statues, talismans, and crystals. They will infuse the fabric object with the essence in their spirit on the way to carry out easy responsibilities the utilization of factors of magic. These cultivated entities were created for the only reason of serving special entities, just so they choose to make themselves useful at all times. They are an out of doors instance of your hobby and the pressure of your life as an extension of you.

Simple spirits have a restricted quantity of energy due to the fact they may be primal elementals and spirits of nature. They have nearly no effect at the reality of the location of the etheric, and they'll be most customarily encountered at the bottom ranges of power. Complex spirits have the electricity to have an impact on validity. In ancient folklore, those spirits have been called elves, fairies, sprites, and demons. The complicated spirits are herbal allies for those who exercise magic. The disembodied human beings aren't some thing greater than the souls of those who are deceased and are each no longer able to delivery on, or they do not need to move on.

The deities of the etheric worldwide are the effective historical entities that human beings have been interacting with and talking with for hundreds of years. They are called gods and goddesses in mythology and folklore. They exist as exquisite fields of complicated attention within the etheric realm. Deities will often show up themselves into human form due to the fact that is the form this is maximum without hassle visible through way of the human eye, and they need to have the ability to talk with humans. You will revel in a broader revel in of popularity and energy while you may make a reference to a deity. While you're gathering electricity from them, they'll additionally be taking power from you, along aspect your mind and feelings, due to the fact that is what gives them their electricity.

Inhabitants of the Astral Planes

When celestial our our bodies skip over from lifestyles on the planet, they go to the astral plane. This is the location this is inhabited via angels, spirits, and immature beings. The astral aircraft is located complete planes above the physical aircraft that is known as earth or the cloth aircraft of being. A heavenly spirit is a being that has been separated from their human shape, despite the fact that they're loose to take a human shape and rejoin the human beings of earth at any time they desire. The astral spirits generally want to address manifestations of their kind of design. You have probable encountered a heavenly being within the direction of a while in the world and not even determined out you had an stumble upon.

The outstanding character you encountered may also were a succubus. When you are viewing the inhabitants of the astral plane, your human eyes are not useful, because of the truth they may be frequently taken in via what they see. A succubus is a stunning introduction that harbors a dark interior. This creature will live up in your invitation to them considering the truth that they select to take the passive direction and assist you to be the aggressor. Then they'll gift themselves because the bodily manifestation of your idea of the proper beauty. When you enter a relationship with a succubus, it will likely be awesome within the starting, however in the long run, the relationship will flip dark because the succubus begins offevolved offevolved to reveal their actual self, however you'll not have the strength to appearance this until you're thus far involved that you feel trapped. Ask the entity without delay in case you need to realise for exceptional if you are handling a succubus. Celestial beings don't have any ability for falsehoods, and they are no longer capable of misinform you.

You possibly encountered a fairy when you have been a little one because kids can with out problems see into the astral aircraft. All of the innocents of the vicinity are true believers, just so they revel in an lively connection to the whole thing they come across on this international. The etheric creatures which might be residing inside the worldwide of the fairies aren't truely satisfied little creatures that fly round on airy wings showing their cute colorings. All of nature is the house of the fairies, and each element this is observed in nature is represented through a fairy. The historic being understood the fairies and believed in them surely. Fairies will luckily coexist with all of the spirits within the astral plane and all of the humans in the international.

Your non secular development and increase can be inhibited via an archon. The non secular strength that radiates off of the lifestyles varieties of the astral aircraft and the earthly aircraft is the meals for those parasitic creatures. Archons are so evil due to the fact they will be angels who've fallen from grace. They attempt to pass themselves off as property of mild and delight regardless of the reality that they're genuinely evil in nature. Archons need to contaminate the whole lot and every body with their evil intentions. They will do some thing in their power to disrupt your religious improvement.

Thought paperwork are the entities that represent each emotion or concept which you have ever skilled in your life. In the astral aircraft, those feelings and mind exist inside the precis shape. The belief-forms within the astral plane will automatically behave with the information that has been infused into them with the aid of the person they were with. All of the concept-office work that you come across at the astral aircraft will fill you with more power and a enjoy of reason. The people, places, and subjects that you see in your dreams are all versions of the idea-forms from the astral planes. You will often engage together with your personal feelings and thoughts. It is crucial that you try to generally remain in a few control of your emotions and mind because of the reality notion bureaucracy will exist in every the bodily international and the astral global. Your wayward mind and immoderate emotions will reason your concept-office work to be totally out of manage.

Seeing Into the Afterlife

Your precise waft of interest will maintain to live on within the astral plane at the same time as you die and depart your physical frame in the back of. This might be your subtle frame, your spirit, or a few a part of your essence this is left in the lower returned of. The beliefs which you maintain at the same time as you're at the physical plane will decide the vacation spot that your identity will take after your loss of life. You would possibly likely skip immediately to one of the astral planes.

You may also start your lifestyles yet again once you are born again into the area, having no conscious memory of the experience you had earlier than. The most important reason that most humans fear demise is that we have no idea what's going to appear to us subsequent. There isn't any actual way to realise that there may be existence beyond the only you are dwelling now. There are reports of people having near-loss of lifestyles reviews in which they describe the top notch slight, the softness, and the lovable sun shades. But the tunnel on the stop of all of this splendor might be not anything extra than the hallway that takes you to the stop of your lifestyles with no longer something beyond that to stay up for.

An atheist could have very top notch perspectives regarding the give up of existence than a person who has a few form of religious notion. The atheist does not believe in God. Therefore moreover they do no longer trust in Heaven as a vacation spot for existence after loss of life. Some human beings count on there can be a opportunity for reincarnation or the selection of persevering with in some shape on an astral plane. The Buddhists do no longer trust that the soul moves on after loss of life however that the man or woman themselves may be reincarnated a brief time once they die. The Hindus furthermore acquire as actual with in reincarnation and the passing on of the soul. The first-rate of the Christians will rely on the specific denomination that they enroll in, however elegant they believe in God as a truth and Heaven as the region that they'll skip when they die.

If you believe that you may flow directly to another plane just like the astral aircraft while you die, then you'll have the possibility of meeting the Masters. Also referred to as the Ascended Masters, they're the spiritually enlightened beings who've moved on from this global, leaving their earthly bodies in the back of for a religious life. They have finished their life cycles and moved beyond the incarnations furnished within the bodily realm. They for the time being are able to stay all the time in the maximum of the astral planes, the Fifth Dimension. When those people have been completing their last incarnation on the planet, they were known as Yogi, Guru, Shaman, or Spiritual master. During their preceding incarnations, they were able to observe all the commands that they needed to discover ways to circulate without delay to that exalted degree. They had been in a function to complete the divine plan which have become set for them and stability out their karmic stability with enough extremely good to wipe out the bad that they had collected of their lives. The Ascended Master may be very near the quantity of the gods. In their new incarnations, they may act as the lecturers for human beings at the equal time as they'll be operating from the spirit realm. They will attend to the non secular needs of humans via inspiring and motivating the spiritual boom of these they choose to assist. Any human can ultimately reap the rank of Ascended Master with the resource of way of following the direction of goodness and accumulating awesome karma in the route of all in their incarnations on the planet.

Reincarnation

When a soul leaves the frame of the deceased person and movements into the frame of a newly born individual, then this is an act of reincarnation. It is also referred to as a rebirth or transmigration. As a spiritual view of existence after dying, it manner that the spirit or the soul of the human will begin a new life in a contemporary shape after they die. The perception in reincarnation is taught as a part of fact through most of the religions of the Far East like Jainism, Buddhism, Sikhism, and Hinduism. The concept inside the lower lower back of reincarnation is that you will input your new shape to be a better character in this unique hazard at lifestyles. You will try to do better than you did within the preceding lifestyles. How you lived your remaining existence will decide how you'll come decrease again for your new life. People who did now not try to act as top, first-rate human beings in their previous lives may work back as a bug or a weed. People who lived as ideal human beings will return to a greater exceptional revel in than the most effective that they had earlier than. The karma that a person collects at some stage in their incarnations will determine what shape their new lifestyles will take. A character who has collected more horrible karma than high-quality karma at some point of their reincarnations will want to keep returning to active existence till they gain karmic balance. Someone with greater terrible karma has no longer found out to stay a righteous lifestyles and allow pass in their ego.

A man or woman will discover salvation after lack of existence when they in the end learn to live the most moral and ethical incarnation that they might stay. The shape of salvation that they're looking for isn't always to be born again, due to the fact this stage of liberation is the actual intention of reincarnation. Coming lower lower back with no end in sight in a unmarried shape after every different isn't always the way most people need to spend eternity. The closing reason of reincarnation is to save you being born over again and entering into the astral plane.

Chapter 5: History of Kundalini Yoga Philosophy

Since time immemorial, humans have been searching for to apprehend their worldwide and control what is in it. Artists have drawn, sang, and written their interpretation of what the Universe is set. Scientists have sunk some of time, energy, and assets into studies; religions have risen and fallen, all to locate the Universe's mystery. Yet however all that try, each day, some component new is decided.

However, most humans overlook to take a look at the most crucial unit of the Universe themselves in a majority of those efforts. You can't apprehend the Universe in case you do no longer recognize your self and haven't unlocked all the innate powers which you maintain inside your self. Kundalini is one of the maximum effective energies of the self. Once locked it lets in an individual to apprehend and enjoy their global in now not possible methods. It permits you to exceed your non secular, highbrow, and physical limits.

The earliest issue out of the phrase Kundalini can be traced to the Vedic writings accrued. These writings were referred to as Upanishads, a word used to intend paying attention to the hold close's teachings at the equal time as sitting down. During such schooling, the novices might in all likelihood reap oral recitations of religious insights thru a draw close at the equal time as sitting down.

During this period, the data factor out that Kundalini changed into an power technological know-how and a divine philosophy. There was no bodily detail of the Kundalini. However, over time, the Upanishads' position have become accompanied because the dependable bodily feature during yogic sports activities. It remains in use in recent times. This yoga changed into in no way taught to everyone or the general public. Kundalini yoga have turn out to be treated as better analyzing for university children who had lengthy past through rigorous coaching to equip their our bodies and minds for the soul and body instructions from their Kundalini masters.

The preference of a follower who might gain information of the era of Kundalini end up executed in utmost secrecy. This follower needed to be from the elite family similarly to possessing unique attributes that set him apart from the rest and which had been assessed via the hold close in secret. Once a worthy candidate became spotted, he might be initiated into the influential Indian Yoga's thriller society.

Kundalini awakening modified right into a thriller stored from the overall public. In truth, practitioners concept they had been doing the general public a decide upon via manner of no longer training them due to the truth; the general public modified into not prepared to deal with the energy that changed into to be aroused in them inside the event that they knew. Such become the secrecy that covered Kundalini yoga exercise.

In the Eleventh Century, the exercising prolonged to Buddhism and Hinduism. Practitioners of those faiths started out to check in Kundalini awakening with an aim to records and unleashing the full-size strength that lies constrained within the human body. In the Fifteenth Century, practitioners of Hatha yoga began out to workout Kundalini awakening. Come the Sixteenth Century, practitioners of Upanishads Yoga started out to study and workout Kundalini awakening.

For a long term after that tapping into Kundalini electricity remained a maintain of the few, especially the Chinese and Indians. They guarded it as a splendid mystery that could most effective be surpassed from a instructor to a praiseworthy and virtually reliable student. Teaching Kundalini or maybe making mentioned the call of the sport of Kundalini awakening became a taboo and attracted a excessive punishment to the wrongdoer of the form of sin. The exercising changed into deemed as best spiritual.

Through their extensively practiced yoga, they experimented with the huge strength that lay limited inside the human frame. These organizations had a usually wealthy religious way of life that sought and although seeks to streamline and purify the human body simply so it can launch Kundalini that is in turn supposed to purpose a exchange of the thoughts. For the Chinese Taoists, to be ushered into religious enlightenment, moreover called the Tao, calls for that one acquire Yin Yang stability in addition to operating toward the microcosmic direction.

Between 1875 and 1961, Carl Jung, a psychiatrist, started a advertising marketing campaign to make Western international places aware of Kundalini and the exceptional power that carries its awakening. Jung's efforts were in large element a achievement because of the reality maximum of the West's hobbies inside the energy can be traced once more to him, in addition to special practitioners.

Jung and people exceptional practitioners had skilled Kundalini awakening and had first-hand facts of approaches the power works. Although its manifestation changed into excellent in each of them and their interpretation of the exercising of Kundalini awakening grow to be specific, they were all jogging from one commonplace floor; that Kundalini become an strength dozing inner the person who might be summoned. They moreover all believed that Kundalini had the potential to beautify religious development in an man or woman, but had to be managed or mastered well.

These influential practitioners got here up with their very private proposals at the exercise of Kundalini awakening. One of those practitioners, George King, asserted that the whole manage of Kundalini via the vertebrae is guy's very last mission within the global. King also tried to interrupt down the Kundalini awakening method whilst bringing up tactics wherein this can be completed as it should be—thru dwelling a well-balanced existence and devoting oneself to serving human beings selflessly.

Because of Jung, King and specific progressives, the 60s have grow to be the remaining decade of improvement for Kundalini know-how. No longer modified into it a preserve of Easterners. Many Westerners have become inquisitive about Kundalini, the manner to rouse it, and meditation in desired. By the Seventies, Kundalini understanding have grow to be even greater well-known as greater human beings have become inquisitive about awakening their innate spiritual and highbrow powers. Driven thru manner of this want, greater humans were professional in awakening Kundalini the proper way as well as recognizing the symptoms and symptoms and symptoms that got here with an awakening.

Currently, Kundalini has been followed and can be stated along many non secular phrases or close to advantageous religious companies, in particular the newly released ones. However, technology however remains skeptical of the entire idea of Kundalini awakening, which quite frankly isn't always any marvel considering technology is greater centered on what may be visible, heard, touched, smelled or tasted. Kundalini is more approximately the sixth revel in and what may be felt.

However, irrespective of its skepticism, even era can not forget about about approximately the accelerated hobby in Kundalini awakening, or the adjustments in human beings who've skilled it display. Scientists, particularly the ones inside the scientific subject, had been analyzing Kundalini to recognize how it is able to be accomplished to treatment and recovery. Some scientific practitioners have inculcated Kundalini yoga into their everyday techniques and workout it of their clinics. A lot of research has additionally prolonged past into identifying the hyperlink amongst intellectual stability and meditation.

The hassle with this haphazard integration of Kundalini into clinical remedy is that now not regularly are the exceptional awakening strategies found. When this occurs, detail-effects to the ones being incorrectly prepared and awoke may be disastrous. There were instances of patients stricken by highbrow and emotional disturbances. Therefore, a few medical personnel have taken this to mean that Kundalini, in elegant, is a unstable workout that need to now not be tried out.

Fortunately, due to the fact the exercise of Kundalini awakening grows, increasingly statistics approximately Kundalini awakening is being disseminated to the overall public. The trouble is that most of the disseminated data speaks to what the awakening is however does no longer skip deeper into the problem, explaining the step-by the usage of-step manner of awakening or what to do later on. You're in ideal fortune due to the fact, on this guide, I've attempted to offer an reason behind those steps in addition to a way to do them thoroughly.

Chapter 6: What Is Kundalini Yoga, and What Are its Goals

Kundalini yoga is a selected yoga exercise designed to rouse, balance, and harmonize Kundalini electricity. Individuals who embark on a Kundalini yoga adventure regularly document that they start experiencing the awakening signs and signs and symptoms and signs and symptoms after without a doubt one or sessions. This awakening furthers as they skip deeper into their Kundalini yoga journey. This yoga form additionally enables manual the Kundalini power, keeping it awoke, whole, and thriving inside the man or woman training it.

Kundalini Yoga

Not all yoga practices are finished in addition. Some are designed to stretch out the physical frame, a few are designed to facilitate a thoughts-body-spirit connection, and others are designed for specific functions, which incorporates Kundalini yoga.

Kundalini yoga does not emphasize the physical as a whole lot as wonderful practices, which includes Hatha yoga. Instead, it includes meditation and mantras as a foundational part of the general practice. The blended experience of the thoughts, body, and spirit being added collectively through those three practices encourages Kundalini awakening and helps Kundalini flow. The frame is supported and awakened with the resource of the yoga poses, the mind is supported and wakened via the mantras, and the spirit is supported and awakened via meditation.

Introduced thru Yogi Bhajan inside the 1970s, Kundalini yoga stays in particular new to the Western regions. It is, however, growing in reputation as extra human beings looking for to contain the thoughts, frame, and spirit connection of their lives.

The Bodies

There are ten our our bodies associated with Kundalini yoga. All ten our our bodies are awakened via Kundalini yoga, allowing people to begin to hold feeling complete Kundalini go along with the go with the flow. These our our bodies are as follows.

The Soul Body

The soul body is your float of spirit. This is in which you connect with your Soul and to infinity. The soul body is considered to be the foundational body and your proper self. It offers you with the functionality to live from your coronary coronary heart. This frame responds to any shape of heart art work, further to the elevating of your Kundalini electricity.

The Negative Mind

Your 2nd body is your terrible thoughts. This is one among our maximum powerful our bodies, as it constantly works in the direction of assessing the environment and events you are in and if there may be any risk present as a stop end result. This body is answerable for your potential to stay alive and objects us with what's regularly referred to as "a longing for belonging," that may be a word coined thru the use of Yogi Bhajan. Your lousy thoughts may be balanced thru integrity and subject.

The Positive Mind

The 1/3 body you've got is your fantastic thoughts. This works closer to assessing what is exquisite, useful, and placing in advance for your environment and occasions. This body lets in you to look in which possibilities lie and in which you'll be capable of get entry to assets. The playful thoughts is chargeable for bringing energy of will and playfulness into your life. Everything you do at the aspect of your navel aspect, or your middle, contributes in your effective thoughts. You also can balance it by way of manner of developing your arrogance.

The Neutral Mind

Your impartial mind is liable for guiding you thru assessing the statistics coming in from each your horrible and excessive great minds. The independent mind is compassionate, acknowledges polarities, and works on intuition. The impartial thoughts can be balanced through meditation, it is a foundational a part of Kundalini yoga.

The Physical Body

Your bodily frame is your temple. This is wherein all the unique 9 our our bodies come collectively to exist in concord. This frame permits you a very good manner to balance yourself and your life. You also can sacrifice for your hopes, desires, and the extra community via your bodily body. The physical frame possesses the strength of the instructor. It is balanced thru normal workout. The physical frame moreover likes to percent what has been discovered out with others.

The Arcline

Your arcline body is shape of a halo that wraps round your head around your earlobes, brow, and hairline. If you're a lady, you have got have been given a 2nd arcline that exists inside the route of your breast line. Your acrline body permits you to intuit the world round you, further to challenge your self upon it. You can use this frame to help you interest and meditate. Any practices associated with the pituitary gland or the 1/three eye (pineal gland) help the arcline body's awakening.

The Aura

Your air of thriller frame is your electromagnetic vicinity of power that extends throughout the bodily body. It is accountable for preserving your lifestyles stress strength and defensive you and offering safety. Through your air of thriller body, you could increase your self every energetically and consciously. Natural fibers are worn at the frame similarly to meditation both contribute to awakening and balancing your air of mystery. You also can include the coloration white into your lifestyles and exercise, which is believed to magnify and make bigger your air of mystery.

The Pranic Body

Your pranic body is supported with the useful resource of your breath, which brings life pressure electricity into your bodily body. This allows you to revel in accomplishment and energy in your life. You have interaction with this frame on every occasion you breathe outside and inside. The pranic body is wakened and supported via pranayama practices.

The Subtle Body

Your ninth body is your diffused frame, and it is chargeable for supporting you be aware beyond the physical remember and into what else exists. This frame is deeply related in your soul frame, because it includes your soul body after your bodily body dies. Many splendid teachers and specialists preserve to educate us via their subtle our our bodies no matter now not being inside the bodily popularity. Your capability to recognize some thing exists inner this body. If you want to experience mastery, do a Kundalini exercise for 1,000 days in a row. Then, your subtle body may be balanced.

The Radiant Body

Your 10th and final body is your radiant frame. This body is responsible for presenting you with radiance, courage, and the Aristocracy. When you meet a person who's glaringly charismatic and magnetic, they've got a balanced, radiant body. To stability and awaken your radiant frame, you want to have dedication. Through the art work of being devoted for your exercising, truth, kindness, and excellence, your balance and wake up your radiant frame.

Embodiment

Though no longer technically a body itself, the embodiment is an essential detail of awakening the ten our our our bodies. Embodiment shows that each one ten our bodies are awakened and balanced. This is the very last goal with Kundalini. When you workout Kundalini yoga, you're awakening, balancing, and strengthening your ten our our our bodies.

Yoga Poses to Awaken the Bodies

The following yoga poses are written inside the collection wherein they ought to be finished. There are 14 poses in normal, all of that are designed that will help you awaken your Kundalini and your 10 our bodies. You want to live privy to your breathing and use each of those as a pose to meditate in. You can also repeat a mantra to help you further combine your thoughts, frame, and spirit.

Easy Pose

Easy pose, called Sukhasana, is the primary pose you are going to start with. This pose calls with a view to take a seat down down at the floor together together with your legs crossed and bringing your palms within the front of your coronary heart. Bringing the hands within the front of the coronary heart in this manner is called the prayer mudra. Rub your arms collectively some times, warming them up. Then, loosen up your thumb joints into your sternum.

Stretch Pose

Gently skip from smooth pose right all the way down to your lower returned, together with your legs stretched directly beneath you and your fingers right away down via your aspects. When you're geared up, bring your heels together and aspect your feet some distance out of your body. Gently raise your head approximately 6 inches off of the ground and look down in the direction of your toes. If this seems like it's miles an excessive amount of or like it's miles bringing ache, you could slide your arms below your lower back and use them to aid you. As you do this, workout the breath of fireside (defined underneath.) Hold this collection for approximately 1–3 mins. If you're pregnant, do not exercise this pose or the breath of fireside.

The breath of fireside is pranayama. To do it, you want to inhale on the equal time as pushing your navel far out of your spine, then exhale, pulling your navel once more towards your spine. This permits you to fill your diaphragm, lungs, and throat with air and then exhale all of the air out of your throat, lungs, and diaphragm.

Knees to Chest Tuck

While laying for your once more, after you finish the stretch pose, you can circulate right right into a knees-to-chest tuck. Simply supply your knees up, wrap your arms round them, after which lightly pull them towards your chest. If you're feeling assured, you could carry your head up. Your nostril need to be pointing among your knees. Use the breath of fire and preserve this option for about 1–3 minutes. If you are pregnant or are experiencing a heavy menstrual cycle, you need to replacement the breath of fireplace of prolonged deep respiratory. Breathe in for about six seconds and out for approximately six seconds. Do now not hold your breath at any detail.

Ego Eradicator

When you're accomplished collectively collectively along with your knees to chest tuck, you want to go back decrease again as much as a seated characteristic collectively in conjunction with your legs crossed inside the front of you. Begin developing the easy pose via bringing your arms again into the prayer mudra within the the front of your chest. Then, curl your fingers in and thing your thumb up in the direction of the air, as in case you are giving a person thumbs up. Your palms should best be gently curled, with the fingertips gently touching the palms and the majority of the fingers last exposed. Then, located your palms up above your head and out to the edges. This opens and exposes your chest and middle. Close your eyes and exercise the breath of fireside for approximately 1–3 mins in advance than moving into the subsequent pose. Again, in case you are pregnant, chorus from the use of the breath of fireplace and as an alternative practice deep breathing.

Hold Your Toes

Now, you need to uncurl your legs and stretch them out to the edges inside the the front of you. Your legs need to be unfold in a huge "V" form within the front of you. Keep your toes flexed at the side of your ft pulled decrease returned within the route of your body. Do no longer push yourself to stretch in addition than is comfortable in this pose. Allow yourself to loosen up into it and be given as authentic with that the more you exercise, the extra bendy you becomes and the less difficult this pose will get. When you are prepared, take a deep inhale and stretch your arms over your head. Then exhale and stretch your arms out to your ft, maintaining onto your ft and a laugh into the pose. Hold this for approximately 1–three minutes.

Grasp Your Shins

Cross your legs yet again, returning to an smooth pose. Hold every of your shins. Then, inhale and flex your spine forward, curling it over as even though to show your once more. When you exhale, flex your spine backward as although to reveal your chest. You have to be getting an tremendous comfortable stretch out of this, so keep it calm and intentional. Do this pose for among 1–3 minutes earlier than transferring straight away to the rock pose.

Rock Pose

To complete the rock pose, you'll want to tuck your toes underneath your self and take a seat on your shins together along with your knees collectively within the front of you. You need to be sitting in your heels in conjunction with your toes cushty. Let your fingers lightly come to a resting function for your thighs in advance than flexing the backbone as you have got been inside the preceding pose. Your eyes should be closed and lightly rolled towards your 1/3 eye in case you experience cushty doing this. Continue this stretching pose for about 1–three mins.

Grasp Your Shoulders

Remain in the identical seated pose as you used for rock pose, along side your heels below you. Keep your torso and head pointed beforehand, looking immediately in the the front of you. When you're prepared, raise your hands up and gently draw near your shoulders together along with your hands. Your left thumb need to be in the back of your left shoulder on the aspect of your arms rested above your left collarbone. Likewise, your right thumb ought to be in the returned of your right shoulder along with your hands rested above your proper collarbone. Sit in this stretch pose for a few moments. Then, on each inhales, twist in the route of the left, and on each exhale, twist toward the proper. Your arms should live lifted, retaining your biceps parallel to the ground in the end of this pose. Do this for 1–3 mins.

To take this pose a step in addition, stay in this posture, go lower back your torso, and head to center, looking without delay in the front of you. Your hands must remain inside the equal position, together with your elbows extended out within the route of the factor. Each time you inhale, convey your elbows up, drawing a line closer to the sky. When you exhale, draw your elbows down, returning to your precise function together together with your biceps parallel to the floor. Do this stretching pose for about 1–3 mins.

Shoulder Lifts

Take some moments to transport again to a crossed leg role. Then, lightly rest your fingers to your knees and allow them to lighten up completely. Refrain from drawing your knees up on this characteristic, as these shoulder lifts can every so often result in tight hips inflicting your knees to draw up in the direction of the sky. Allow them to loosen up in the direction of the ground as an opportunity. When you're prepared, inhale and raise the left shoulder closer to the sky. As you exhale, lower the left shoulder and simultaneously carry the proper shoulder. Continue this for 1 minute before reversing the manner. As you reverse it, convey your right shoulder at the inhale, and drop it to beautify your left shoulder on the exhale. Continue the stretch on this aspect for every specific 1 minute.

Double Shoulder Lifts

After finishing your alternating shoulder lifts, you may start lifting every shoulders on the identical time. For this, you want to raise them and attempt to pull them toward each different on the inhale. Then, drop them and push them a protracted way from every particular, letting them loosen up at the exhale. Continue doing this double shoulder enhance exercise for 1 minute.

Turn Your Head

As you continue to hold the smooth pose at the side of your legs crossed inside the the front of you and your fingers rested lightly on your knees, you may start turning your head. This will stretch out your neck, pinnacle backbone, and better once more location, allowing you to revel in a pleasant, exciting sensation. Each time you inhale, turn your head to the left. When you exhale, flip your head to the proper. Your head must live level, and your nostril should draw a line round your head this is parallel to the floor. After you have got have been given finished this for one minute, contrary the breath. On each inhalation, turn your head to the proper, and at the exhalation, draw your nostril at some stage in the the the front of you, turning your head inside the route of the left. When you're completed with this reversed breathing part of the pose, convey your head to return returned lower returned again to a resting function in the front of you, slowly exhale, and lighten up your body.

Frog Pose

This may be one of the extra advanced poses of the yoga consultation. The frog pose calls on the way to stand up right into a squatting function, resting to your ft. Your heels ought to be drawn up within the direction of the sky and touching each extremely good below you. Your fingertips can be positioned on the ground amongst your knees, together together with your palms separated tremendous and each tip firmly planted into the floor. Evenly displace the burden among each of your fingers and toes to allow for a targeted pose. Your head have to be lifted alongside facet your chin pointing upward, permitting you to gaze inside the direction of the sky. Don't deliver your head too tough, however as an alternative permit for a nice cushty upward recognition. As you inhale, stretch your legs out barely allowing your glutes to upward push in the direction of the sky. Remain in your toes for this pose. As you exhale, come all the way down to the particular function. Continue keeping this rhythm with your breath for approximately fifty 4 repetitions. However, if that is beyond your capabilities diploma, you may constantly purpose for thirteen to 26 repetitions. Continue collectively with extra for your workout whenever until you reach the fifty 4 repetition mark.

Laya Yoga Meditation

With maximum of your poses now completed, you can input the meditation a part of the method. Here, you want to sit down down decrease once more into the clean pose — Left your wrists to relaxation in your knees as you component your palms inside the direction of the sky. Then, supply the top of your thumb to the surrender of your index finger and create a round shape. This is known as the Gyan mudra. Now, chant the subsequent mantra. As you are chanting, make the effort to visualize electricity that spirals out of your backbone's base to the pinnacle of your head. This is the observed out strength of Kundalini.

The chant is as follows:

- "Ek Ong Karah,

- Saa Taa Naa Maah

- Siree Whaah, Hay Guroo."

You need to hold chanting and meditating for a whole of eleven minutes to enjoy the entire effect of this manner. Carry the visualization from the bottom of your spine to the pinnacle of your head during the whole device, allowing it to spread really in a few component manner it manifests for you. Refrain from forcing the electricity, but as an opportunity set the purpose and permit it to reveal you the way it wants to be observed out, in preference to the opportunity way round. This is an awesome possibility to find out the exercise of liberating blocks by way of using allowing the approach to unfold.

Savasana

Lastly, you want to prevent your Kundalini yoga series with a savasana pose. This pose calls with a purpose to gently lie all the way down to your lower again, together along with your ft down and lightly separated and your hands snug out for your elements. Breathe deliberately but with a natural rhythm right proper here and loosen up due to the fact the energies flow thru your frame. Instead of seeking to create or pressure something, get hold of all that comes your way. This will will permit you to combine the whole yoga enjoy. You can gently manual your interest between the 10 our our bodies, stability, and wholeness from this pose.

Chapter 7: What Is Kundalini and What It Wakens

In the previous bankruptcy, you've got been given a glimpse of what Kundalini Awakening may be. This monetary ruin is dedicated definitely to Kundalini Awakening. You will study what it's miles, what strategies are used to rouse it (every spontaneously and consciously), the symptoms that you are probable to experience, and what it looks like.

So, to reiterate, Kundalini is the woman modern strength lying latent (inside the shape of a coiled snake) at the bottom of the spine in each one oldsters. However, there may be no bodily evidence of the presence of this snake-like detail in our bodies. It is a diffused power shape you have got the power to evoke and comprehend its presence at the equal time as you enjoy its power.

Like prana and the nadis or channels via which it flows, Kundalini is invisible to the human eye however can be felt and professional whilst it is in its energetic nation. This subtle form of strength carries different elements of our non-bodily self, such as our active imprints, natural and purchased varieties of energies, and emotional imprints. Kundalini is the location in which our existence research, collectively with the ones created with the aid of the usage of our family, subculture, and society (together known as "samskara" in Sanskrit).

Interestingly, even though the strength contained in our Kundalini appears metaphorical, or perhaps metaphysical to novices, you may rest assured that it is not. Kundalini is subtle but virtually does exist and is some element that lots folks are capable of activating and awakening the usage of a whole lot of strategies, including meditation, yoga and others.

You can enjoy the Kundalini electricity the identical manner you could experience your pores and skin or see a few component colourful through your eyes. You can enjoy Kundalini power dance up and down thru your backbone and the nadis to your frame within the wakened state. As it movements freely, you may moreover enjoy the dissolution of all of the strength blockages in your body. As the exceptional blockages of electricity accrued over the years are released, your perception into prolonged-held ideals is progressed, and you can see topics in a clearer shape than in advance than.

Most professionals are sure to agree that awakening the Kundalini with out guru guidance can be risky, each for you and the human beings round you. Kundalini awakening can display up both through the aware exercise of yoga, meditation, and specific techniques and a give up end result of trauma, near-loss of life experience, a debilitating infection, in dreams, misuse, and abuse of drugs or perhaps thru having intercourse with a companion with an woke up Kundalini. Awakening the Kundalini requires awesome levels of the organization area of our frame and mind so we may be geared up to simply accept the responsibilities that accompany the strength of waking up the innate Kundalini.

So, why should anyone try and awaken the Kundalini Shakti? Ultimately awakening the Kundalini journeys lower back to God, or the conventional divine electricity. It permits to take away your ego, too, as you surrender yourself to the time-commemorated divinity. The very last motive of Kundalini awakening is for self-recognition.

Yes, the awakening of Kundalini may probably appear like a crazy enjoy that would lead you to conditions beyond human control. Yet, this is most effective a part of the method. Kundalini is, in reality, an herbal and smart technique with a systematic motive on the surrender.

An awoke Kundalini allows you untie all of the emotional and intellectual knots in your thoughts so you can see the right cause of your lifestyles, in particular, and the Universe, in famous. The awakening of the Kundalini is the growing of Shakti interior you. It moreover manner the route for Shiva to go into you is getting cleared and prepared.

Kundalini awakening way Shakti is asking out to Shiva to return down and meet Her even as She climbs up to meet Him. Kundalini Awakening is an workout to supply divinity into our materialistic international greater than trying to cross past our existence. Kundalini Awakening is a device of purifying our body, mind, and soul so we grow to be boxes prepared to accumulate and hold the traditional divine power inside us.

Kundalini Awakening is frequently visible as a divine revelation as it comes with a huge wide variety of mystical opinions like connectedness with the complete Universe, bliss, beautiful sunglasses and lighting fixtures, and notion of past-human planes of cognizance. The fact, seemingly, is that Kundalini Awakening is not anything more than step considered one of an prolonged journey lower back to in that you come from. When you wake up the dormant, sound asleep Shakti, the real artwork is quite plenty to begin.

If you've got lengthy past through spiritual healing and purification, then it would be a smooth and no longer-so-hard transition that takes place at the same time as the Kundalini awakens. However, if the Shakti awakens in advance than you're geared up or in a hurry, the enjoy may be quite unpleasant.

Effectively, while the Kundalini awakens, it's miles like waking up a napping large or giantess, in this situation. She will purify your body, coronary coronary heart, and mind. However, when you have the Kundalini earlier than coping with the problems and precise unsightly factors of your existence, then the "cleansing" method can hit you difficult. Therefore, you mustn't pressure the awakening of the

Kundalini. Let Her awaken in Her very personal time at the same time as She is aware of you're prepared to simply accept Her within the lively u.S. Of the us.

The manner of purification preferred earlier than the Kundalini Shakti is woken up can be tough and immoderate. You may need to be hospitalized or even institutionalized, as it may be quite disorienting to live in the materialistic international with a completely awoke Kundalini. Once She wakes up, then your global will in no way be the equal.

Therefore, if you are eager on awakening the Kundalini Shakti lying latent in you, then make sure you without a doubt recognize its capability impact. Understand how deep your dreams are, and apprehend that the course will not be easy. Finally, remind your self that you can face a scenario in that you choice you hadn't woken HER up in case you do awaken the Kundalini.

Awakening the Kundalini Shakti is not pretty lots psychic powers and bliss and oneness with the Universe. It is likewise the hard work concerned inside the spiritual route. However, once SHE is big unsleeping, she is on top of things, and you could best do what you need to do. So, decide after very well wondering subjects thru.

Chapter 8: Kundalini Yoga the Supreme Knowledge

Kundalini Yoga is one in each of the faculties of yoga that focuses on awakening Kundalini energy in a person's frame with the useful useful resource of strolling within the route of asanas (postures), pranayama (respiratory techniques), meditation, and chanting of mantras. It seeks to nurture and cultivate people' spiritual potential and their innate capability to talk the truth, uphold values and preserve the compassion and awareness had to heal and serve. As a person practices Kundalini Yoga, he can release and unfastened himself from karma and discover and apprehend his lifestyles's cause or Dharma.

The exercise of Kundalini Yoga, additionally called the "yoga of hobby," interests to rouse and arouse the dormant and napping Kundalini strength, which many accept as true with is coiled at the lowest of the backbone. The aim is to fire up the coiled strength to get to the bottom of and make its manner up thru the seven chakras that live inside the spine until it reaches and penetrates the seventh or crown chakra.

Performing and operating towards physical video games and breathing techniques, and meditation in Kundalini Yoga are crucial in making organized the body, the thoughts, and the nervous system to handle the Kundalini power because it awakens and starts offevolved ascending from the bottom of the backbone to the crown chakra. Most of the bodily sports and postures targeted in particular at the navel and resolution region. Another essential reputation in this college of yoga are respiration strategies. Asanas or postures performed in Kundalini Yoga are done with particular pranayama or breathing techniques that motive to heighten the poses' effects. Poses and sequences are regularly carried out rapidly and repetitively, collectively with a chosen method of respiratory. Other times, poses are held for nice durations at the same time as breathing in a selected manner. These practices free up the Kundalini power this is residing at the bottom of the spine, permitting it to tour upwards towards the top's crown finally.

Before someone can bask in the slight and splendor of the Kundalini energy, he need to first undergo a period of rigorous cleansing and purification and strength and conditioning the body and the concerned system. He need to be the form of character who possesses a corporation and stable moral basis. His values and ideals need to be robust and unyielding. He ought to have a sure degree of area that is not without problems shaken and shattered. A character who seeks religious and Kundalini awakening need to have handiest the purest purpose of searching out and unraveling his actual capability. He must stroll inside the course with an open coronary coronary heart and an open thoughts.

Kundalini Yoga is one of the most secure strategies to evoke the Kundalini. Through austere Yogic sports activities like pranayama, breath manipulate, asanas or postures, meditation, and mantra chanting, someone's body, thoughts, and spirit are organized to cope with manipulate the arising Kundalini electricity.

The technique of spiritual and Kundalini awakening is some thing that you need to method with extraordinary care and recognize. Although absolutely everyone has the Kundalini inner, rousing it with the wrong intentions can pleasant bring a person more harm than correct. The act of awakening want to stem from a herbal coronary heart. It have to be a heart that seeks no longer some thing however oneness with the Divine. A coronary coronary heart aspires and intends to use the powers that encompass an awakened Kundalini for the greater top. It want to be a coronary heart this is open, compassionate, actual, and kind. It ought to be a coronary heart that seeks to heal and to serve.

Yoga for religious and Kundalini awakening should be employed and practiced in a loving manner of offering the self; the existence forces and energies are launched, liberated, and freed up in an clean, harmonious and stable manner.

How to Increase the Potential of Your Body and Mind with the Kundalini Yoga

Being capable of do it for your very very very own is exactly what this e-book is ready. However, if you need to do it with a spiritual draw close or guru's assist, then this will contain complete willpower and submission for your draw close. Your grasp also can require you to do effective meditation practices; but, some claim an high-quality manner to evoke one's Kundalini so long as the disciple relinquishes the whole thing and submits to his/her maintain near. The hassle right here is that it isn't easy to find out a actual grasp. Unfortunately, there are such masses of people on hand who declare to be a master however are, in truth, genuinely merely complete of hacks and shams. Another problem with this technique is that even though a grasp can be capable of awaken your Kundalini, your soul won't be equipped for it. This refers to your non secular adulthood. Therefore, on the subject of awakening the Kundalini, it is strongly advocated that you do the paintings yourself in reality so your soul can mature and make you be prepared for it. Of direction, you're despite the truth that unfastened to invite help from a grasp but do not overlook your private religious increase.

It might be secure to expect that your Kundalini lies dormant within the root of your spinal column right now, explaining why you are analyzing this ebook. Do no longer fear, as this ebook will manual you and educate you the techniques with a view to let you awaken the serpentine electricity. Just live with me to advantage statistics as you look at me in this adventure of real Kundalini awakening.

Releasing is a effective workout in an effort to will let you awaken your Kundalini strength even more as it prevents you from constricting your electricity and ultimate the gap wherein

Kundalini power desires to go together with the float.

Acceptance Equals Flow

As a part of our human conditioning, permitting matters to truly display up with out at once leaping proper right into a worry-primarily based completely need to govern the whole lot can be tough. We have a tendency to love topics performed a amazing way and often keep in mind that inside the occasion that they don't occur the "proper" way, that we are in some way doomed. Many individuals may additionally moreover even revel in a sensation much like that of a fear of loss of existence at the same time as matters do now not circulate in accordance to plan.

You ought to apprehend that attractiveness straight away equals waft strength on the subject of life and lifestyles-pressure strength. Using float energy to help your awakening will not best equate to a more awakening experience, but it will moreover translate into much less worry. Many humans normally normally generally tend to try and face up to because of fear, and in flip, they immediately make their awakening painful. This is due to the fact they war to virtually float and alternatively sense as even though they should manipulate everything.

When you feel as even though your awakening is painful, it is probable due to the truth you're resisting the go along with the go with the flow of the power. Imagine maintaining a bottle of soda and shaking it. The quantity of strain (energy) internal of the bottle may hastily upward thrust. Unless you removed the lid, it would have nowhere to go. As such, it'd probably result in the bottle feeling very bloated and difficult to the touch. Imagine this being your self. When you select out out to rouse Kundalini energy after which restriction the glide via refusing to clearly be given topics, you turn out to be crushed with strength inner. The bloated and hard feeling that the soda bottle should have felt like may, for you, feel like pain and excessive electricity. You can also moreover revel in like a volcano, even!

When you accept topics as they will be, it turns into loads less tough as a way to release the need to be on top of factors and allow subjects to show up truely. Then, you could have a more high-quality revel in with Kundalini energy, as opposed to feeling as despite the fact that you are being ploughed down by way of way of intense energy buildup.

Releasing Fear

The first step to permitting subjects to waft is releasing worry. Fear is the strength that motives us to restrict. When we sense scared of a few aspect, we might also anxious up, try and reduce the quantity of area we absorb, or perhaps begin shaking. Our our bodies turn out to be masses closed and our strength even extra closed. If you live chronically in this kingdom, or if you right now change into this nation because of your awakening signs and signs and symptoms and signs and signs and symptoms, you could emerge as feeling very overwhelmed thru everything.

Releasing worry also can seem tough, but it's far much less hard than you suspect. A tremendous manner to launch worry is to surely lay on your mattress as a minimum more than one instances a day and permit energy to transport thru you. Invite the energy to easy away a few issue that doesn't belong internal you, and that isn't serving you for your revel in. This will assist worry strength flow into out of you and a more effective shape of woke up Kundalini electricity waft through you.

Any time you revel in fear springing up, without a doubt take a second to invite your energies to easy themselves out. Take a while to phrase what goes on inner you. You may even use this as an possibility to make the effort to apply a respiration meditation to help launch any strength inside you and loosen up greater. Anything that allows you to release fear and pick out love and popularity will assist immensely together together with your awakening technique.

Releasing Daily Expectations

Many human beings upward push with expectations on how our day goes to play out. When our expectations aren't met, or a few component does now not flow to plan, we end up feeling very dissatisfied and confused out. This is an extreme form of stress that can effects be avoided with the aid of manner of releasing each day expectations.

When you wake inside the morning, take inventory of what "goals" to arise. For example, perhaps you need to visit art work or a medical doctor's appointment. Then, launch expectations on everything else. Release expectancies on how the ones sports will play out. Release expectancies on what website on line visitors may be like, whether or not or no longer or not you may don't forget to carry the entirety with you, and what's going to take place in among. Instead, permit your self to want for the terrific and do your top notch, however release expectancies that the entirety will take place flawlessly each time.

Releasing People that Bring You Pain

One of the components of awakening that many people find out quite challenging is freeing people from your life. You have probably been keeping at once to many people for your lifestyles that don't wholesome nicely. Many of the humans we normally generally tend to maintain in our lives whilst we aren't running from an woke up u.S.A. Will be predisposed to be poisonous. Even despite the fact that we may love them or feel obligated to hold them in our lives, this doesn't advise that they've a right to our courting. You need to recall that you do no longer owe everyone some aspect. If the man or woman in question is a person you can't keep away from, say a coworker or a md, and there may be sincerely no longer some thing you can do approximately it inside the right away second, you need to limit touch as an lousy lot as feasible.

Releasing Places that Bring You Pain

In addition to human beings that could bring you pain, you could additionally discover which you will be predisposed to maintain frequenting locations that supply you pain. These won't be obvious pains, but if they create you discomfort or displeasure, you could assure that they create a few diploma of struggling or ache.

The most common locations humans commonplace that can carry ache into their lives embody locations like:

• Excessively busy grocery shops, or grocery stores that constantly sell horrible first-rate components

• Your place of business

• A family member or pal's house (frequently because of feelings of duty)

• The mall, or one of a type places to "grasp out" that carry you soreness

- A doctor or therapist's place of work in which you do now not sense supported with the useful aid of the medical health practitioner or therapist

There are many one of a kind places that you'll be able to don't forget to your private as well. These places all percentage one issue in common: they create about approximately pain or displeasure. Often, but, we tend to revel in obligated to keep going to these locations for one purpose or a few other. While you can need to visit comparable places, this does not suggest you have to visit the appropriate locations that supply you pain or displeasure virtually due to the reality you have got usually finished that. You can discover a new grocery shop this is a laugh and that sells better awesome food. You can find out a brand new place of business or lease a modern medical health practitioner or therapist, in region of frequenting locations that don't carry peace and contentment into your lifestyles. You do no longer need to hold out in places that maintain you uncomfortable.

Ultimately, we commonly normally have a tendency to spend a number of time within the ones locations due to the truth human conditioning leads us to trust that we are imagined to do that. Then, we find ourselves annoyed and confused out because of the fact the ones locations do no longer please us. However, we not regularly get into the inspiration reason of the trouble and find out new practices! Take a while to take into account any place for your existence that reasons any degree of struggling, and take away those places or trade them out for places that supply pleasure and contentment into your lifestyles.

Releasing Old Cycles that Restrict Your Awakening

Humans are creatures of dependancy. Nearly the whole thing we do is completed in a round movement or in cycles. Being privy to the ones cycles and disposing of them is a effective way to get rid of ourselves from toxic cycles which is probably no longer serving our nicely being. When we take a second to deal with the ones cycles and select out otherwise, we empower ourselves to behave in any other case. This manner we are able to begin taking over new cycles which may be more aligned with our nicely-being.

Some commonplace cycles we typically will be predisposed to revel in however no longer recognize are individuals who turn out to be routine. For instance, say someone says some element to you that triggers a bully from your kids as soon as said. So, you proper now begin feeling unhappy about your self and who you're. Then, you begin feeling disempowered. You could likely flip to a comforting exercise, including eating, smoking, consuming, lying in bed, or in reality something else as a means to attempt to comfort your self from the ache. Then, once you consolation yourself, you resume your each day life. When the trigger is pulled again at a later date, you start the cycle all all over again.

These cycles can consume us. As properly, they not frequently serve us in any manner. In many instances, the cycles themselves are related to stuff that took place long within the beyond. Sometimes, we've already healed from the reason, but the cycle is so ordinary that we preserve to apply it and never make an effort to launch it and update it with a current day cycle.

Anywhere which you observe behavior like this taking region, make an effort to recall why those behavior exist and the way you can go approximately decreasing or eliminating them. Releasing terrible cycles that deliver vain struggling must have a really notable effect on your recuperation, in addition to on helping your Kundalini awakening.

Chapter 9: Physical, Mental and Sexual Benefits of Kundalini Yoga Practice

Clearing and Calming of the Mind

As with any exercise which includes meditation, the ones practices will truely clean your thoughts. When you allow yourself to meditate as a minimum 15 minutes an afternoon, you'll see that even if you had a racing thoughts, it'd begin to sit lower back out. This is a gain that most humans will discover useful, even if beginning with the Kundalini awakening approach.

Improvement in Memory

With the mixture of the pranayamas and yoga poses, you may be introducing extra oxygen into your device. This, in turn, permits the blood to glide extra without troubles all through the frame, which encompass the mind. More blood getting into the thoughts improves the cognitive functions and the pituitary and pineal glands.

Physical Ailments Can be Relieved or Cured

During the approach of Kundalini awakening, you are running in the route of cleansing out your nadis and chakras to facilitate Kundalini Shakti's movement. This cleansing brings approximately an environment in your body that diseases cannot continue to exist, so they will be substantially decreased or eliminated.

Increased Physical and Mental Strength

There isn't any doubt that the dutiful workout of yoga poses gets you into form. Coupled with the opportunity bodily activities in Kundalini, your thoughts turns into sharper and focused, which in turn will increase your intellectual fortitude. You will find out that you may be capable of control your feelings, as well.

Proven Build Up of Willpower

There isn't always any doubt that some of those Kundalini sports activities activities are hard. There are a few that you'll be looking to practice extraordinary carrying activities earlier than you even reflect onconsideration on graduating yourself. With the need to preserve to push yourself systematically strengthens your power of mind and drives you to succeed.

Feeling One with the Universe

When you can hook up with the better energies interior your self, you may recognize that we're all definitely from the identical deliver. No rely variety what your historical past, schooling, upbringing, belief tool, or marital reputation, we're based totally within the same electricity of the Ultimate Consciousness.

Tap into Inner Intuition and Guides

As you dig deeper within yourself and can silence your mind, you may begin to pay hobby every other voice that lets in you to in no way steer you wrong. This inner manual is your intuition, your gut feeling, which continuously has your higher pastimes at coronary heart. Learn to accept as genuine with this voice, and you could excel more fast during the Kundalini awakening approach.

Emotional Balance

Because you have reinforced your frame and cleared your thoughts, frame, and soul of troubling additives that have befell to you, this makes you extra on top of factors of your emotions, and you will discover you surely will not react as loads, if the least bit. You recognise what the bigger photograph is, and you do no longer allow petty matters to interrupt your day.

Feeling Overall Bliss and Peace

When you undergo the Kundalini awakening manner, there in reality are low factors. However, genuinely as rapid, you can be sent as a whole lot as soaring heights which blow your thoughts. You can't even don't forget this united states of america at this element for your journey. Feeling the ones feelings truely makes up for any hardships you can undergo.

Psychic Abilities Are Enhanced

You will find out that you turns into more sensitive to the sounds, colorations, and vibrations round you. This occurs whilst you come more in tune together together with your body after which it radiates from there. When your instinct will become extra extra exquisite, you may begin to understand the whole lot that you want in the intervening time that you want it.

Slower Aging Process

When you get to the higher ranges of Kundalini yoga workout, you'll see a glow as a manner to start to reveal on your pores and pores and skin. This is in part because of the cleaning approach. It is likewise because of the reality you are balancing out the factors internal your frame to feature greater successfully. Your frame will no longer need to paintings so tough in retaining itself.

Connection with the Divine

This is the final intention of Kundalini yoga and awakening. When you'll be in direct reference to the writer, some thing is possible. You lose all earthly bounds and are able to reap the so-referred to as unachievable. Going back to the Source is the appropriate prize for all of the hard paintings and resolution you have got were given located into your workout.

Sacred Chant

Many of the chakras can be healed via a sacred chant. When you use a mantra, rhythm, and breath, it's been determined to have beneficial effects on nicely-being and fitness. It also can supply delight to the coronary heart and the soul. The sacred sound is referred to as Naad Yoga. The enjoy comes from how your voice's vibrations may also have a pleasing effect on the frame, the mind, and the spirit. In reality, the sound can exchange the chemical substances in your mind.

Inner Soul Guidance

Through Kundalini Awakening and Kundalini Yoga, you can check all about the electricity of your intuitive mind. As we cited earlier than, you want to learn how to listen to the voice indoors your head. Each person has this voice, however it's far as an entire lot as you to pick out to take note of it. As you easy your mind, specifically your unconscious thoughts, you'll discover ways to listen to your mind even as no longer having to depend upon others. This manner, you could continuously be gift and revel in your intuition. The extra you exercise, the more potent your capability to stand alternatives and alternatives will come!

Karma

It is belief that it takes you out of the karma cycle whilst you workout Kundalini. As you start to workout, your top notch goal will expand, consequently putting you into Kundalini Kriyas. These are sporting activities that help you burn off karma. As you exercise extra, you will become greater intuitive to your choices similarly in your conscious. As you do this, you will start to stroll on a Dharma course in area of residing steady with karma.

Spiritual Chain

As you currently recognize, Kundalini has been taught for lots of years. Originally, it changed into taught through the Master to the pupil. In a Kundalini Yoga elegance, you could chant, "Ong Namo Guru Dev Namo." As you do this, you will be associated with non secular masters from the instances earlier than your lifestyles. The lineage is referred to as The Golden Chain. Through religious awareness, it's going to assure Kundalini's teachings to ensure you can stay unadulterated and herbal.

Emotional Balance

What you may no longer understand is that through balancing your Kundalini, you can moreover be balancing your glands, purifying your blood, strengthening your disturbing tool, and cleansing out your unconscious. As you wake up your Kundalini, you'll advantage the energy to select how you respond to your mind and feelings as opposed to without a doubt reacting. You can certainly have a more recognition all through your every day sports activities. As you exercising extra, you'll also discover ways to allow your emotions skip. No longer will you in truth react emotionally? By growing a independent thoughts, you could discover your self dwelling a extra first rate lifestyles. The secret is to act in preference to reacting.

No More Negativity

As you exercise awakening your Kundalini, you will begin to expand your air of mystery. This is the electricity vicinity that surrounds you. Its primary venture is to offer you with a warning of any great or bad feelings round you. At this point, you probably have a susceptible air of secrecy. When it is willing, you can resultseasily allow terrible affects to have an impact on you. As you enhance your aura, it will keep you targeted, and you can recognize your real identification.

New Lifestyle

In life, we make numerous excuses that maintain us sad. Luckily, Kundalini Yoga is meant for humans with busy lives. That method that it is able to be completed speedy and although paintings effectively. It is a yoga that could healthful into many one of a kind existence. Whether you attend weekly or bi-weekly, there are various benefits to be determined. There also are yoga teachings which could change different factors of your existence. Whether you need to alternate your hygiene, little one-rearing, or aware communication, there is yoga for that!

Relax

As we referred to in advance, Kundalini yoga will paintings to enhance your disturbing device. If your fearful device is prone at this aspect, you're in all likelihood liable to strain. Through yoga, you may learn how to loosen up like you have in no manner felt in advance than. You may also additionally locate that you'll obtain a rejuvenating kingdom through yoga to carry you to standard rest. Through ordinary exercise, it permit you to gather resilience to pressure and provide you with a few extra stamina.

Community

On your journey, you do not need to try this by myself. Often, yoga brings humans together who're like-minded. This may be a completely effective tool as you tour alongside your interest journey. If you weren't already conscious, many Kundalini yoga centers and studios might also additionally want to assist welcome you right right into a community. With exceptional human beings, you could extend a network which can meditate and chant collectively. It additionally enables to have humans that will help you make immoderate fine changes in your life.

Befriending Your Soul

As you exercise Kundalini, you could begin to get a grip for your ego. You will slowly be discovered about your soul's depth so that you may have a take a look at the reality of your connection to your soul and the Universe. Through extra exercise, you may learn how to unite yourself with the Infinite. Gaining the revel in can help you overlook your insecurities of expertise who you're. This way, you could let skip of the past and healthily display up your destiny.

Chapter 10: What Are the Chakras?

Chakras are the power centers of the frame. If the physical body has vital organs, then the spiritual or power frame has chakras. It is important to hold your chakras healthful, as dangerous chakras could bring about terrible physical health. According to a look at, in advance than bodily ailments manifest at the physical body, they first seem at the strength or spiritual body. The chakras are also points in which electricity can enter and depart the body. To awaken the Kundalini, you need to have sturdy and wholesome chakras.

Since there may be a hyperlink the various strength frame and the physical frame, you want to ensure that your chakras are clean and healthful. The chakras, specially the principle chakras of the frame, facilitate the unfastened go together with the waft of energy. When someone is sick, he's maximum probably to have some issues with one or more of his chakras.

It should be stated that the chakras do not really relate on your bodily body, however they also can have an effect on your life. For example, having a strong root chakra may also imply that you have balance in lifestyles. If you've got got a healthful heart chakra, then the opportunities are that your life is entire of harmony and love. As you could see, your chakras' reputation and fitness ought to have a significant have an effect on on your existence.

Psychic energy additionally may be received through growing the chakras. Therefore, taking walks on your chakras can be an critical a part of your schooling. Now, it should be referred to that the frame has seven fundamental chakras. These seven chakras are decided alongside the backbone, starting from the base of the spine and as much as the crown chakra, placed some inches above the pinnacle. Let us talk them separately.

The seven Chakras

The First Chakra— Root Chakras

The base chakra is the begin of the lively adventure in the subtle frame. Its Sanskrit name technique "root." It is the Earth element. It is survival. It is the right "To Have." It is proper here that the Kundalini strength is stored. This is the location of physical fitness, grounded-ness, stability, younger quality, power, combat or flight intuition, and prosperity.

This chakra is associated with the colour purple. It is placed at the bottom of the backbone and carries the power there and surrounding the legs, feet, and gonads. It is mounted for your experience of scent, the primary revel in you are aware about even as you are born.

When your root chakra is balanced, you'll experience stable, sufficient, cushty with yourself, focused, calm, grounded, and associated with nature and the earth.

When your root chakra is imbalanced, you may revel in feelings of loss of confidence, anger, disconnection, depression, scarcity of staying energy, anxiety, greed, useless worry, and absence. When this imbalance manifests in our bodily our our bodies, it could seem as not unusual contamination, weight problems, eating troubles, constipation, knee problems, sciatica, or maybe hemorrhoids.

Since the muse chakra is wherein the dormant Kundalini power lives and rises from at the identical time as woke up, it's miles essential to apprehend the chakra's trends and its connection to all of the particular chakras. However, one need to now not emphasize this power and here is why: Kundalini awakening starts offevolved right here, but it can additionally forestall in the root chakra. Some memories show that it is able to be the very last chakra to genuinely awaken. The relaxation of the transformation through the chakras also can stand up first however for proper balance to be achieved, Kundalini's strength have to pass lower back to the start to in which the supply of the electricity awakening began.

The Second Chakra — Svadhisthana

The second chakra is also regularly known as the sacral chakra. Its Sanskrit call way "sweetness." It is the detail of Water. It is the area of emotion and sexuality. It is the proper "To Feel." This is the area of satisfaction, fluid motion, creativity, and passion.

This chakra is related to the coloration orange and is positioned in the region truely under the navel for your decrease stomach and is associated with the bladder, female reproductive organs, lymphatic machine, and pelvis. It is mounted to the revel in of flavor.

When your sacral chakra is balanced, you may revel in glad, cushty, revolutionary, passionate, and capable of connecting bodily. This is also wherein the stress to procreate exists.

When your sacral chakra is imbalanced, you can sense unworthy, isolated, numb, stiff, overly sensitive, and emotional. You may additionally have a sexual dependancy, or what is known as sexual anorexia, hormone imbalance, and potential for miscarriages or problem conceiving.

This is an area in that you block your emotions. Here is in which you could restriction the flow of electricity as a whole. It is important to do the emotional artwork vital, getting better out of vicinity feelings and sometimes re-experiencing them so you can heal and release them as you preserve your awakening adventure. Ultimately, even as you heal and unblock your sacral chakra, you could permit a healthy go together with the glide of your emotional power so that you can enjoy delight thru body motion and sexuality. Unblocking your sacral chakra can will permit you to revel in change, boom, and reference to your passionate self.

The Third Chakra — Manipura

The 1/three chakra is likewise called the sun plexus chakra. Its Sanskrit call method "lustrous gem." It is the detail of Fire. It is electricity, and it's far energy. It is the proper "To Act." This is the place of personal power, the electricity of will, and the experience of cause.

This chakra is related to the coloration yellow, and it's far located between the place absolutely below the navel and the bottom of the sternum. The bodily function associated with the solar chakra is the adrenal glands. Your adrenal glands alter metabolism, blood stress, and your immune tool.

When the chakra is in stability, you will experience energy and pressure, self perception, a feel of respect for others, in addition to understand for the self, an lively and comfortable disposition, and a sturdy revel in of reason.

An imbalance of the solar plexus chakra can represent as an boastful demeanor, disturbing thoughts-set, overbearing sensibilities, and addictions. The opposite factor of imbalance should look like a deficiency of electricity, helplessness, a sense of weak point, timidity, and a submissive existence technique.

This chakra demonstrates a good sized turning thing in Kundalini awakening. It will purpose a profound shift in your intentions, intuitions, self-rate, and ability to appearance the beauty within the international. This is wherein judgment, biases, and prejudice soften away, first with the self and then the entire international round you. This is in that you start to experience your Kundalini energy, however there can be even though a lot extra to go through.

The Fourth Chakra — Anahata

The fourth chakra is also referred to as the heart chakra. The Sanskrit call for this chakra interprets to mean "unstuck," or unharmed, unbeaten. It is the element of Air. It is love and relationships. It is the right "To Love." This is the region of compassion for the self and others, recognition of the self and others, and stability in all relationships.

When the coronary heart chakra is in stability, you may sense love, compassion, interconnectedness, popularity; lifestyles will drift smoothly. There can be a favored feeling of love for each person and the whole thing— Universal love.

If the coronary heart chakra is imbalanced, it could explicit this through excessiveness or deficiency. A awful coronary coronary heart chakra can often appear to be low self confidence or low self-esteem, depression, isolation, depression, incapacity to breathe deeply. Excessive coronary coronary heart chakra strength suggests itself in the form of co-dependency, clingy conduct, and an excessive amount of caretaking of others.

Interestingly, like with the extremes indexed above, the coronary heart chakra can spontaneously open for energetic go together with the waft from a newly professional, deep love of someone. On the alternative give up, excessive loss or grief can cause a shift and crack open.

Regardless of what reasons the initial awakening of the coronary coronary heart chakra, be it the Kundalini awakening technique, falling in love, or grieving a loss, it's far extraordinary to be an emotional roller-coaster. This can be aided with the Kundalini practices referred to in this ebook.

The Fifth Chakra — Vishuddhi

The 5th chakra is likewise referred to as the throat chakra. The Sanskrit call for this chakra translated is "purification." It is the element of Ether or sound. It is communique. It is the proper "To Speak." This is the region of self-expression, speaking, soul track, and the capacity to talk with others.

The shade associated with this chakra is blue, and it's far located at the throat.

Several physical functions are connected to this chakra, which includes the already referred to throat, jaw, neck, thyroid gland, tooth, ears, and esophagus; the entirety is related to talking and listening.

When this chakra is balanced, you can experience clean and trustworthy self-expression, honest and properly conversation, innovative expression, and affinity with self and others. There is also an functionality to recognize the stability of opposite forces with reverence, accepting the price of every mild and darkish, immoderate and coffee, and that they each have a vital function inside the harmony of all lifestyles electricity.

When this chakra testimonies imbalances or blockages, it may take region as hassle expressing oneself, lack of potential to release wounds, ache or trauma due to suppressed feelings, sore throat, hassle listening to, actual ear problems, tight neck and shoulders, and stagnant progressive flow.

This chakra has a superb deal to do with sound, such a lot of strategies for clearing blockages or organising and activating the throat chakra make use of making a tune or chanting, rhythm entrainment, and sound vibration.

The Sixth Chakra — Ajna

The 6th chakra is frequently known as the forehead chakra or 0.33 eye. The Sanskrit call for this chakra interprets to intend "understand" or to apprehend. It is the detail of Light. It is seen perception, intuition, clairvoyance. It is the right "To See." This is the vicinity of creativeness, notion, telepathy, vision, rational pinnacle judgment.

The sixth chakra is associated with the colour indigo and is located a number of the eyes or behind the eyebrows. Its bodily attribute is the pituitary and pineal gland. The pituitary gland regulates hormone secretions, on the identical time because the pineal gland regulates sleep styles and circadian rhythms.

When the sixth chakra is balanced, there are wonderful competencies in belief, your mind is comfy and might method perception speedy, improved reminiscence and intelligence, lacking worry of demise, you have were given a strong connection for your intuition. You should have clairvoyant and telepathic competencies floor.

An imbalance within the sixth chakra can arise as headaches, highbrow fitness issues, and illnesses which encompass hallucinations and nightmares, paranoia, anxiety, and delusions. Because of its connection to sight and the eyes, it is able to additionally present itself as terrible sight or visible belief.

Once this chakra turns into open and blockages begin to easy, power can tour go into reverse thru the lower chakras for persisted healing and cleaning, as there'll possibly be unresolved strength blocks however looking cleansing. That is why the Kundalini awakening gadget is an ongoing adventure with the self.

The Seventh Chakra — Sahasrara

The seventh chakra is also frequently referred to as the crown chakra. The Sanskrit call for this chakra interprets to mean "thousand-fold." It is the detail of concept. It is progressed interest. It is the proper "To Know." This is the vicinity of information, of enlightenment.

The crown chakra is associated with the coloration violet and is placed at the top of the cerebral cortex's head. This chakra's bodily difficulty covered the mind, arms, apprehensive device, and in detail the pituitary gland, developing a hyperlink to the 6th chakra.

When the seventh chakra is balanced, you will have an prolonged reputation at the manner to cause a transcendence of barriers projected through the usage of humanity and the criminal tips of nature, have a extra records and recognition of loss of lifestyles, mortality, and the immortality of the soul, extended and heightened non secular presents and capabilities, and the advent of miracles.

If your crown chakra is blocked, it could arise as migraines, headaches, and fashionable anxiety round the head. You can also enjoy alienated or remoted, go through boredom, have an apathetic notable, disconnection, and shortage comprehension or ability to analyze and preserve new facts. It also can flow into inside the route of being a piece spacey, "to your head" all the time, and once in a while overly highbrow, preventing your potential to reap herbal-recognition.

The balancing or beginning of this chakra in Kundalini awakening is closely connected to the 1/three eye. The functionality to go beyond and enjoy enlightenment is the shifting a ways from smaller styles to welcome a deeper, broader angle, one which encompasses all life and all depend, past the confines of restrained mind and ideals that preserve our kundalini locked and dormant.

From the Root to the Head and Beyond

The machine as an entire is a cute, throbbing and constantly vibrating energetic life pressure of its very very own. This chakra strength is generally gift and constantly fluctuating. When the Kundalini strength is activated at the lowest of your backbone to your first chakra, you begin the upward adventure with a view to reason you to face all the elements, functions, blocks, deficiencies, and excesses of your chakras. It is the begin of recovery and awakening in your divine moderate and energy to turn out to be one with the strength of advent. What you find out on this path, the course via the chakras is probably how you return into touch with the real nature of yourself and all subjects.

Knowing approximately every chakra is vital for the awakening device because it will give you the statistics to pay attention for your frame. It is also essential due to the fact they may be the vital, active a part of your being right now associated with Kundalini awakening experience. Take some time to concentrate to each part of your frame, each chakra machine, and broaden a relationship to every power so you may be connected to the whole of your diffused body.

How to Clear and Balance the Chakras

Try allowing one week of consciousness for each chakra and pay interest along the way to whether or not or no longer or no longer you want to provide greater, or an lousy lot lots less time, to every electricity. Your body is continuously speakme to you. Listen to it.

Root Chakra: Muladhara

Your root chakra is established to the detail Earth. One terrific way to help easy the strength to your root is to be in nature. Think approximately tree roots. Where do tree roots want to be? In the wooded place, within the soil, close to the rivers and streams, inside the mountains. Healing your root chakra includes a connection to nature. Take off your shoes and walk alongside the seaside. Find a secluded nature direction and spend time attaining out and touching flora, timber, moss, and soil. Go on a camping experience and stay inside the woods for more than one days. While you are there, acquire a few nature treasures like stones, feathers, driftwood, and mosses to take home. Find a location in your house and create a nature altar.

If you could't make it out to the woods or stay in a town with out a number of nature get entry to, visit your close by nursery or garden center and walk spherical in it. Get some potted houseplants to take home and make part of your international. Find out what the plant life want and need and usually tend to them.

Your root chakra is likewise the shade pink. You can do a whole lot of electricity clearing thru running with and the usage of the colour red. Grow or acquire pink vegetation to enhance your own home. Dress your body in shade purple with a pink outfit, headband, or other accents.

Construct an altar to the coloration pink the use of purple candles, embellishes, or paintings you want, and mild the candles every day to honor your root chakra.

www.ingramcontent.com/pod-product-compliance
Lightning Source LLC
Chambersburg PA
CBHW071443080526
44587CB00014B/1973